BUSINESS CONTINUITY
STRATEGIES

BUSINESS CONTINUITY STRATEGIES

PROTECTING AGAINST UNPLANNED DISASTERS

3rd Edition

KENNETH N. MYERS

WILEY

JOHN WILEY & SONS, INC.

Previous editions are as follows:
Total Contingency Planning for Disasters: Managing Risks, Minimizing Loss, Ensuring Business Continuity, ISBN 0-471-15379-6.
Manager's Guide to Contingency Planning and Disasters: Protecting Vital Facilities and Critical Operations 2nd Edition, ISBN 0-471-35835-X.

Library of Congress Cataloging-in-Publication Data

Myers, Kenneth N., 1932–
Business continuity strategies : protecting against unplanned disasters / Kenneth N. Myers.
   p. cm.
Rev. ed. of: Manager's guide to contingency planning for disasters. 2nd ed. c1999.
Includes index.
ISBN-13: 978-0-470-04038-6 (cloth)
ISBN-10: 0-470-04038-6 (cloth)
1. Crisis management.   2. Strategic planning.   3. Risk assessment.   I. Myers, Kenneth N., 1932–
Manager's guide to contingency planning for disasters.   II. Title.

HD49.M93 2006
658.4'056—dc22   2006046217

Printed in the United States of America

10 9 8 7 6 5 4 3 2 1

To Marcia

CONTENTS

ABOUT THE AUTHOR

Kenneth N. Myers is an internationally recognized contingency planning specialist and educator. He has developed business continuity strategies for leading organizations in the United States, Europe, Mexico, and Puerto Rico. Mr. Myers developed the curricula and was the course leader for business continuity strategies to protect against unplanned disasters seminars for The Battelle Institute and The American Management Association and was called to consult with the largest tenant in the World Trade Center following its bombing. In this book, he presents a **new contingency program paradigm** reflecting the latest in contingency strategies development thinking as well as the impact of terrorism and workplace violence on business continuity needs. He is also the author of *Manager's Guide to Contingency Planning for Disasters: Protecting Vital Facilities and Critical Operations* and *Total Contingency Planning for Disasters: Managing Risk . . . Minimizing Loss . . . Ensuring Business Continuity.*

PREFACE

The increase in terrorism and workplace violence has emphasized the need to develop business continuity strategies to protect against unplanned disasters.

Kenneth Myers, one of the foremost innovators and educators in contingency planning, presents a new contingency program paradigm urging boards of directors to take a proactive role in insisting organizations institutionalize policies aimed at preventing workplace violence. Mr. Myers documents employer workplace violence liabilities; describes the three stages of conduct prior to a workplace violence incident; and recommends supervisory training to prevent workplace violence.

Mr. Myers explains why many existing disaster recovery plans are inordinately detailed and too costly to fund and maintain. He also presents a methodology for transitioning to a contingency program that is more cost-effective and more realistic. He also describes why Human Resources is the discipline best positioned to develop and administer business contingency programs.

This book presents organizations that have multiple locations with a template for planning, developing, and administering contingency programs consistent in purpose, scope, strategy, and level of detail. It also provides guidelines and controls to contain development costs and to ensure low-cost interim processing strategies, consistent with the low probability of a disaster.

Mr. Myers also documents 30 recommendations by the National Institute of Standards and Technology (NIST) following an investigation of the collapse of the World Trade Center in New York City. These recommendations address: increased structural integrity; enhanced fire endurance; improved fire resistance; increased fire protection; improved emergency response; and improved evacuation procedures for mobility-impaired building occupants.

1

DEFINING THE PROBLEM

BUSINESS CONTINUITY CONCERNS

Common areas of exposure to a disaster for a business include:

- Telephone communications
- Computer processing
- Vital facilities
- Critical operations

Telephone Communications

Telephones are often taken for granted; they are seldom out of service except for brief periods, such as immediately following a storm. Older electromechanical telephone switching equipment was extremely reliable. However, consumer demand for more sophisticated service has resulted in a conversion from electromechanical to software-controlled switching systems. The advantage of such systems is that they are easily modified to provide more sophisticated options to customers. The downside is increased vulnerability to periodic interruptions in telephone service owing to software malfunction. Every time computer software is changed, the risk of error increases—error that may lie dormant for months until the weakness is exposed. Moreover, it is unrealistic to expect all software changes to be sufficiently tested to preclude failure. Many of the features are new, and models for testing are, by definition, incomplete. Therefore, it is appropriate to prepare a contingency program that will provide minimum voice communication capability during a stabilization period.

1

Computer Processing

Financial service organizations cannot operate for more than a day or two without computer processing, as they need this capability to service transactions.

Yet for many other organizations, this is not the case. Although many businesses are dependent on computers for day-to-day operations, it is incorrect to assume that they could not operate without this support during a relatively brief disaster recovery period that might last a week or two. The difficult part is focusing on the right issue—keeping the business running, rather than keeping the computer running.

Operating without Computer Processing Capability

Manufacturers can be exposed to several problems if computer processing is inoperable. However, careful analysis usually concludes that although inefficient, product still can be manufactured and shipped without normal computer processing support. Alternate interim processing strategies and prerequisites for manufacturing without normal computer support need to be negotiated with functional managers. Prerequisites, such as starting points, need to be included in the contingency program to ensure that they will be available when needed. For example, it is not that storeroom inventories cannot be updated without an on-line computer; the problem is lack of a "starting point" or, in other words, a record of what the inventory file looked like when the computer outage occurred. So if a prevention program includes daily responsibility to store off-site a duplicate copy of the storeroom inventory file, immediately following a computer disaster the file could be printed at another location and delivered to manufacturing as a snapshot of inventory locations and availability. Receipts and disbursements could easily be updated with a simple personal computer (PC) spreadsheet until normal computer processing is restored. See Exhibit 1.1 for vital manufacturing support functions.

Headquarters operations can also be exposed to problems if computer processing is suddenly inoperable. However, careful analysis again usually concludes that although inefficient, business still can continue and customers can still be serviced without normal computer processing support. It helps to look at administrative business functions and what alternatives are available to get the job done without computer processing.

EXHIBIT 1.1   Vital Manufacturing Support Functions

- Take orders
- Schedule production
- Order material
- Receive and store material
- Control inventory
- Pick items
- Manufacture
- Ship
- Invoice

Insurance providers are concerned about issues such as new business underwriting; determining "in force" for claims adjudication; beneficiary information; and exposure for coverage that would have been canceled under normal circumstances. In each of these instances, there are alternative strategies that, although inefficient and cumbersome, can be used to ensure business continuity until computer processing is restored.

Distributors need strategies for taking and processing orders that are normally entered into computer databases, identifying kitting requirements, producing picking documents, inventory management, producing shipping documentation, and handling returns. The question to be asked is not "What problems would you have?"; it is "If confronted with this situation, what would you do to maintain market share and service customers until normal operations resume?"

Associations and agencies are concerned about membership services, legislation and public policy, publications, research, education and training, call centers, and government regulations. In most instances, the overriding consideration is to seek solutions for operating temporarily without normal computer processing capability that will not require continual funding, such as a computer hot-site agreement, but would ensure continuity in servicing members, volunteers, and staff during a stabilization period.

Interim processing strategies for meeting administrative responsibilities without normal computer support need to be negotiated with department managers. The window of *expected* outage must be determined. For the most part, information systems managers consistently agree that they could restore computer processing capability within 10 working days (14 calendar days). So the question to be asked of department managers is not "How long can you do without . . ." or "What do you need . . ."; managers tend to understate and pad the first question, and in response to the second question tend to ask for more than they need. Both questions beg answers and initiate thought processes that are not conducive to cost-effective contingency programs and invite discussions and deliberations that require further documentation and maintenance expense. The only question to ask line managers in relation to doing without normal computer processing is "What alternate strategies could be used to continue functioning for approximately ten days without computer processing capability?" When *that* question is asked, 99 percent of the responses are positive, that is, department managers are willing to accept operating at less than 100 percent efficiency and admit what could be done to meet the challenge of temporarily working without computer processing.

The simple psychology and willingness of contingency planners to "stick their necks out" and insist on establishing a reasonable limit to an expected computer outage will, in turn, have the positive effect of persuading line managers to admit how they could survive. Establishing this "window" up front is the key to a collaborative solution. But also remember that in establishing the window, information systems managers must also accept some risk and not pad their expected recovery capability. The question is not "When are they absolutely positive beyond any reasonable doubt that computer processing will be restored?"; rather, it is "Given emergency conditions, working 24 hours a day, seven days a week, with adequate resources, when is it likely that computer processing could be restored?" On-line connectivity can wait because there are other solutions available, but being able to process data is the important requirement. See Exhibit 1.2 for a list of typical administrative business functions.

Computer processing problems could be caused by a myriad of conditions. Power grids could fail due to unanticipated drops in demand (as users of questionable systems delay initializing operations, either because corrective work has not been completed or because of other concerns) which are so severe that the power companies must bring down and reconfigure power systems grids nationally. Failures of

EXHIBIT 1.2   Typical Administrative Business Functions

- Inventory management
- Order processing
- Scheduling
- Billing
- Receivables
- Payables
- General accounting
- Payroll
- Human resources
- Data processing

satellite communications, HVAC (heating, ventilation, air conditioning, and cooling) systems, automated processing equipment, and computer hardware or software are all possible. The broad and diversified nature of this potential problem is such that testing cannot ensure that some systems might not fail.

One-time potential problem issues have two dimensions. The first is to identify steps that need to be taken to reduce the likelihood of computer-dependent operations from being interrupted and monitoring compliance with those programs, within reason. Without careful oversight by informed senior management, this approach can wind up being a boondoggle for consulting firms—fear tactics, an inordinate amount of "analysis" and "weigh it by the pound" reports, endless meetings, and a large consulting bill.

Most important, however, is to develop a fallback plan that will ensure business continuity even if computer-dependent operations are temporarily inoperable. Experience and common sense suggest that a fallback plan is the safety net that needs to be in place, and organizations that already have a facility contingency program already have one. It just needs to be dusted off and modified slightly, and it can easily be used as a fallback plan. Conversely, if an organization does not already have a contingency program for loss of computer processing, now is the time to prepare one because it will solve both problems. Chances are that if there are failures, they will be isolated and will be corrected in a matter of days, if not hours. See Exhibit 1.3 for a fallback plan development strategy.

EXHIBIT 1.3   Computer Processing Fallback Plan Development Strategy

- Identify computer-dependent vendors and services.
- Identify business functions dependent on computer processing.
- Fund and monitor a prevention program.
- Obtain senior management's approval of a corporate policy and strategy for a fallback plan.
- Develop "what if" interim processing strategies for all potentially affected business functions to protect market share and support customer service, even if normal computing capability is not available for a few days.
- Add a prevention program.
- Add an incident recovery plan.

Vital Facilities

The loss of buildings resulting from fire and other accidents is not a new threat. Nor are there any miraculous solutions. Insurance is still the most cost-effective answer. Business failure following a disaster is normally caused by a loss of assets, such as a manufacturing facility, distribution center, or office building, or an inability to support vital business functions following a disruption in normal processing capability. An inability to support vital business functions immediately following a publicized disaster can be devastating when this information is in the hands of competitors. If orders are "lost," customer service communications lines are inoperable, or inventory availability records become unreliable, even if only for a few days, it can result in a significant loss of market share, particularly with the 20 percent of a company's customers who make up 80 percent of its revenue. Most organizations have not adequately addressed the issue of how to keep the business running if a plant or office building is inaccessible for several days. In other words, the concern is not what to do if assets are destroyed, but how to continue to operate a business if primary work locations are temporarily inaccessible or unusable.

In many production and manufacturing facilities, losing normal computer processing capability would have a serious impact on efficiency, order processing, scheduling, and tracking orders, but it would not destroy the ability to somehow manually shepherd product through the manufacturing and shipping process. Efficiency would suffer; record keeping would become a nightmare, excess inventory would have to be ordered (and worked off later) to avoid stock-outs, and production rates would drop, but product would get out the door.

Losing access to an entire production facility or one critical operation could, in many instances, bring manufacturing to a halt. Without alternate solutions to ship product until operations return to normal, business failure could result. It is this possibility and its impact on cash flow that demands that companies have contingency programs for loss of normal computer processing capability and "what if" strategies for a temporary loss of access to production facilities.

Raw material and component parts might be sent to alternate manufacturing sources; components might be purchased instead of manufactured; excess regional production capacities might be temporarily leased; "second-choice" production alternatives might be approved; inspection and quality control procedures might be changed; and some items might be shipped direct. The important issue is for manufacturing managers to take the time to "think through" which alternatives are most likely to work and which are most cost-effective. It is important that these alternate production methods or "what if" strategies be documented in writing so that: (1) their workability can be validated annually; (2) any prerequisites, such as maintaining daily backup copies of inventory status reports or files off-site to support alternate manufacturing methods, can be identified and inserted into a prevention plan; and (3) crisis management activities, such as using the most recent stock status reports as a basis for insurance claims, are added to the incident recovery plan.

Only a Computer Recovery Plan

Which comes first, the chicken or the egg? Which comes first in contingency planning? Recovering lost technology or keeping the business running? *The business continuity program should come first.* In fact, data processing plans to recover technology that are developed before interim processing strategies are explored normally result in an excessive amount of resources committed to redundant computer processing capability. Auditors are becoming increasingly critical of the lack of business continuity programs and are beginning to emphasize this area more than the loss of computer processing technology. After all, what good is a restored computer if users are unable to keep the business running immediately following a disaster? If you are just getting started in contingency planning, you should address the business continuity issue *before* you worry about redundant computer processing capability.

Current Program May Not Work

Less than 25 percent of business organizations have a workable contingency program. Some programs look good on paper—but would not work if they had to be implemented. Programs that are not viable usually have three things in common:

1. The focus is on keeping the computer running rather than on keeping the business running.
2. No one has taken the time to identify alternate procedures to support functions that *normally* rely on computer technology but could actually survive a stabilization period using alternate methods.
3. The program contains unnecessary detail and professes to cope with problems that are typically nonexistent.

Exhibit 1.4 lists common reasons why many contingency programs will not work.

EXHIBIT 1.4   Common Disaster Recovery Plan Problems

- Focus on recovering computer technology at costly hot sites, rather than on sustaining business continuity until temporary computer processing capability can be restored locally
- Lack an awareness and education program that enables functional managers to understand the importance of their input and are willing to participate in program development
- Do not explore alternate procedures that could sustain vital business functions (that normally are dependent on centralized computer processing) until computer processing capability is restored
- Provide excessively detailed procedures when guidelines are all that are needed

---

CHARACTERISTICS OF A SOUND PROGRAM

A contingency program should be reviewed annually to ensure compatibility with business practices and to integrate lessons learned from new disasters and test results into more cost-effective solutions. Many times it is helpful to have someone other than the individual who developed the program to conduct such a review. It is difficult to be objective when reviewing your own work.

A *corporate contingency program* approved by senior management is a requirement. This document should emphasize that (1) providing 100 percent redundancy for all types of physical disasters is simply not practical; (2) documenting detailed alternate procedures for an infinite number of combinations of possible disasters is also not realistic and would create a "monster" to maintain; and (3) departmental managers are the architects of "what if" interim processing strategies that will serve as guidelines to ensure business continuity following a disaster.

Assumptions under which a program is developed should be stated to clarify expectations and avoid excessive documentation. Examples of assumptions include:

- Qualified personnel will be available to execute the program.
- Healthcare agencies and institutions will be operational.
- A building evacuation plan exists.
- Inefficiencies are expected during a stabilization period.
- Incoming telephone calls will be rerouted within two hours.

A prevention program should reflect disaster prevention responsibilities; ongoing education and training requirements; testing programs; other sound risk management practices; and any additional measures required to support relocation strategies, interim processing strategies, or technology restoration plans. The primary purpose of a prevention program is to reduce the likelihood of a disaster, such as physical security programs, and to take steps that will minimize impact, such as storing computer files off-site, if a disaster does occur.

An incident response plan should ensure an organized response to a facility-related disaster and provide for the rapid rerouting of incoming phone calls and a strategy for restoring computer processing capability. It also includes relocation strategies, minimum staff required during a stabilization period following a facility disaster, notification for personnel and customers, damage assessment, and media management.

Interim processing strategies, in the absence of other instructions, will be used to maintain business continuity if facilities become inaccessible following a facility disaster. Emphasis is on retaining market share, servicing customers, and maintaining cash flow. Business continuity strategies should have been developed by discussions with department managers familiar with existing business practices and alternative options. These strategies should also include functioning without normal computer support (computer operations may not be restored for days) and with minimum staff if relocation is needed.

COST-REDUCTION OPPORTUNITIES

The most costly mistake that a business can make in developing its program is to have it aimed at keeping technology running instead of keeping the *business* running (Exhibit 1.5 provides an action plan for cost savings). Contingency programs that are *not* cost-effective usually have three characteristics:

1. Program focus is on keeping technology running rather than on keeping the business running.
2. No one worked with functional supervisors to develop alternate procedures to support vital business functions until normal processing capability is restored.
3. The program fails to recognize that businesses could continue to function for a week or two without normal computer processing capability.

Cost-reduction opportunities exist due to individual mistakes that alone sound innocuous but, in combination with other related mistakes, spell bad financial judgment. First, an error in interpretation of the Foreign Corrupt Practices Act by accounting firms led to criticizing clients for "lack of a computer disaster recovery plan." That criticism was misdirected. What was actually needed was interim

---

EXHIBIT 1.5   Action Plan for Cost Savings

- Initiate a cost reduction project.
- Have outside specialists (other than those who developed the existing plan) conduct a plan evaluation.
- Focus only on sustaining cash flow and servicing customers during a disaster recovery period.
- Deal with business functions, *never* with computer systems.
- Work with functional line managers and first-line supervisors to analyze options.
- Develop cost-effective guidelines that will sustain vital business functions.

---

processing strategies to be used in the event of a disruption in normal data processing technology. Placing undue emphasis on computer technology, instead of business continuity, was the mistake. Because the focus was on the wrong issue, it led organizations to assign project responsibility to the wrong department. Had the objective been business continuity, project responsibility might have been assigned to a staff person positioned to facilitate a strategic plan. However, with the focus on computers, responsibility was assigned to data processing personnel, who are normally not trained in the synergistic process used to develop strategic programs.

In many instances, these errors resulted in technical solutions being substituted for sound business judgment because the situation was defined as a computer problem that needed a computer solution. The result for many organizations has been excessive expenditures for redundant processing. Taken over a period of 20 to 30 years, this amounts to millions of dollars being wasted. Exhibit 1.6 provides a brief synopsis of why cost-reduction opportunities exist.

EXHIBIT 1.6   Why Cost-Reduction Opportunities Exist

- Initial program focused on getting the computer running quickly at costly computer hot sites rather than waiting a few more days to restore operation at a cold site
- Plan development responsibility assigned to data processing rather than to a staff position
- Lack of specialized problem-solving process that continually links the low probability of occurrence with the need for cost-effective solutions

---

How to Contain Program Development Costs

Minimizing contingency program development costs centers on five interconnected issues: (1) plan development sequence, (2) mind-set, (3) assumptions, (4) communications, and (5) a specialized problem-solving process. If any are missing or not dealt with appropriately, development costs will be excessive, the end product will not be of good quality, and it will take forever to complete the project.

Plan development sequence means positioning and selling senior management on a corporate contingency planning policy and strategy, and documenting this corporate policy and strategy in writing *before any other activities are undertaken in the program development process.* If this is not the first step, then problem-solving practices are used, which are totally inappropriate. For instance, conducting a "business impact analysis" to determine what is critical *under normal conditions* is unproductive. A definition of *critical* is needed. In a contingency planning context, critical is not what receives the highest priority under normal operating conditions because we are not worried about operating under normal conditions. We are concerned about which business functions will be so impaired as to threaten business continuity following a disaster because they lack alternate strategies to operate under those conditions. What is critical at the time a physical disaster occurs depends on what alternative strategies can be used to support that business function. If a particular business function has alternative methods to service customers for a two-week period when computer processing is inoperable, then there is nothing critical because business continuity is not threatened.

The worst mistake is to begin a contingency program project by developing a computer recovery plan based on an assumption that the business could not operate for two weeks without normal computer support and that prioritizes application recovery based on the wrong definition of critical, as described in the last paragraph. It takes someone with seasoned contingency program experience to prevail in establishing the proper development sequence. The benefit, however, is that a program can be completed in 30 days and at a fraction of the cost.

Mind-set is the philosophy under which a contingency program is developed, and failure to document the proper mind-set in a corporate contingency planning policy and strategy will result in false starts, lack of cooperation, and unnecessary expense. For instance, the objective of the program should be "survival," not "business as usual," immediately following a physical disaster because the latter demands ongoing expenditures that annually take away from the bottom line and are not justified given the low probability of a disaster. A more cost-effective mind-set is to reduce or eliminate reoccurring expenditures, such as computer hot-site fees and testing, and instead authorize expenditures on an as-needed basis when and if a disaster actually occurs.

Remember that a contingency program is only a reference document. Managers will decide specifically what to do at the time a disaster occurs, depending on how much damage is done and what the prognosis is for reentering the building.

Communicating effectively can have an impact on completing a contingency program on a timely basis. Repeated communication of corporate contingency program policy and strategy to senior executives, department managers and key supervisors, and to staff developing a program is extremely beneficial. (Remember, individuals quite often do not comprehend information presented only once.) It constantly reminds them of the need to control program development costs, presents a "road map" that keeps them on the path to timely completion, and acts as a deterrent to a natural tendency by everyone to include too much detail.

Contingency planning for disasters requires a different problem-solving process than is used to solve other business problems because of the low probability of a disruption to business continuity due to a physical disaster. Traditional problem-solving techniques used by most consultants and corporate staff involve lengthy fact-finding studies, as well as addressing and resolving issues in painstaking detail. This is because the problems being addressed will affect the everyday operation of a business. This is not true for a facility contingency program. Because it is extremely unlikely that a serious disaster will ever affect a specific site, there is no justification for lengthy studies to gain consensus on what is most critical or for formulating detailed plans. Interim processing strategies need to be documented for all business functions regardless of their relative criticality, and detailed documentation is inappropriate. The contingency planning process is a specialized strategic planning methodology designed to address this need and

EXHIBIT 1.7   Guide to Contain Program Development Costs

- Prepare a program development "road map."
- Assume a mind-set to minimize program development costs.
- Document assumptions on which a program is based.
- Communicate often to executives and line managers.
- Authorize a program development process designed to minimize program development costs and enable a prototype program to be completed in 30 days.
- Use internal resources to roll out a prototype program to other locations.

to minimize program development costs. See Exhibit 1.7 for a guide to contain program development costs.

Where to Look for Cost Reductions in an Existing Computer Disaster Recovery Plan

For organizations with a computer disaster recovery plan, there are three areas that should be examined:

1. Plan maintenance
2. Backup computer hot-site subscription fees
3. Backup computer hot-site testing

Exhibit 1.8 indicates major areas that should be investigated for cost reductions.

EXHIBIT 1.8   Where to Look for Cost Reductions

- Maintenance
- Scope
- Amount of detail
- Documentation structure
- Backup communications
- Cumulative cost of backup processing subscription fees over a 20- to 30-year period
- Testing costs, including disruption to normal duties

Plan Maintenance

Maintenance expenses are directly related to the volume of material, level of detail, and documentation format. A great deal of "Do we really need to include this?" kind of thinking is required when a program is under development or being evaluated. If this approach is not taken, issues that should be left out will be included, thus adding unnecessarily to maintenance costs. The objective is to leave out of a program those issues that can be dealt with at the time a disaster occurs or that cannot be specified until the impact of a specific disaster has been assessed. Remember that the specifics of many emergency response activities cannot be determined until after damage assessment of a specific disaster or incident.

Preparing a quality program that clearly and concisely addresses only relevant issues requires considerable experience, good business orientation, and a structured format. One problem is that most software documentation packages demand detail that is not needed; in fact, it gets in the way of doing a good job.

Hot-Site Subscription Fees

Backup computer hot-site requirements should be examined for cost-reduction potential. In today's cost-sensitive business environment, computer hot-site and cold-site subscription fees can be a source for large, ongoing cost reductions.

For most organizations, other than banks and communications providers, backup computer contracts with hot-site vendors are a waste of money. They are not needed, because in a crisis such as a disaster, a computer operation usually can be restored within a one- to two-week period somewhere, somehow, and most functional supervisors can find other ways to keep vital business functions running until processing capability can be restored.

Testing

The cost of resources tied up in the testing of backup computer hot-site operations can be considerable. The cost of planning, preparing for tests, scheduling, arranging transportation, testing, evaluation of results, and sustaining corrective action programs can drain an organization of resources that should be used to address daily operating requirements.

Audit Concerns

Auditors are becoming increasingly concerned about the viability of contingency programs (Exhibit 1.9 lists some of these concerns). Because the data processing department is an organization's focal point of information technology and the department most conspicuously vulnerable to a disaster, management most often looks to data processing personnel to develop data center restoration and application recovery programs. This approach is *not* appropriate for developing "what if" interim processing strategies.

Data Center Restoration and Application Recovery

The data processing department should address data center restoration and application recovery; however, the development of interim processing strategies is best accomplished by specially trained professionals.

Developing "What If" Interim Processing Strategies

The heart of any worthwhile program is the development of interim processing strategies. This requires awareness and education and involves a highly specialized problem-solving process. In most instances, it is not realistic to expect in-house personnel (data processing or any other department) to serve in this role. Effective interim processing strategies are not a data processing problem; they are a corporate issue, requiring an organizationwide problem-solving process.

EXHIBIT 1.9   Audit Concerns

- Lack of awareness and education
- Department managers not sufficiently involved in developing alternate procedures
- Contains unnecessary detail
- Not testable
- Technology oriented rather than business oriented
- Not cost-effective

Involving Department Managers

The most serious mistake is to develop alternate strategies for how specific administrative functions or manufacturing operations will operate during a stabilization period following a disaster, without the understanding and support of line managers who would have to use them following a facility disaster. Department managers are the only ones who have the knowledge of what alternate strategies might be both workable and practical. They are also the ones with on-the-job knowledge that can be most creative and resourceful in analyzing these options. The way that department managers are approached about participating in developing a facility contingency program can make the difference between cooperation in searching for cost-effective solutions or protecting their own interests. Most department managers are overworked and have to be selective about what projects take up their valuable time. They focus on getting things done and, as a result, have little time for a strategic planning project like helping to develop interim processing strategies, particularly for a theoretical disaster that is unlikely to happen.

Department managers need to be dealt with carefully and respectfully if their cooperation is expected. Conduct executive briefings specifically for them. Keep the briefings concise, no longer than 30 minutes. Explain the company's exposure to a facility disaster; explain that such a disaster might affect the company's ability to stay in business and that alternate strategies to service customers and maintain market share need to be developed. Windows of expected outages for operating without normal computer processing support and the building's inaccessibility should be resolved ahead of time and discussed in the briefing. Never ask "How long could you do without?" because it causes the department managers to go on the defensive, rather than being cooperative because they have no frame of reference (window of expected outage) within which to be creative. This is a crucial step because windows of expected outage psychologically permit department managers to "get their arms around the problem" and deal with it in a positive manner.

If windows of expected outages are not stated up front, department

EXHIBIT 1.10   Involving Department Managers

- Conduct briefings for department managers.
- Explain exposure to business continuity.
- Describe expected outage windows for computer processing and building accessibility.
- Take notes on alternate interim processing strategies.
- Summarize business continuity strategies.
- Obtain department manager's approval.

managers will be unwilling to stick their necks out to develop alternate strategies because the problem statement is too broad. Finally, do not ask department managers to write anything down. The individual developing the program should take notes and summarize the managers' suggestions in short concise statements, with no editorializing or detailing "how" they will be done. The capabilities and judgments of the department managers are adequate, and anyway, the "how" will depend on the specific nature of a disaster, and no one knows exactly what that will be. Interim processing strategies should be reviewed and approved by the department managers. See Exhibit 1.10 for involving department managers.

NEED FOR COST-EFFECTIVE SOLUTIONS

The low probability of a disaster means an obligation to search for the lowest-cost solution. It does not make economic sense to allocate the same level of resources to solve a problem that has a high probability of happening as one that will probably never occur. If you do not continually make a strong case for this mind-set, it will be forgotten, and well-intentioned individuals will select solutions that are sophisticated and costly. It is easy to rationalize expenditures conceptualized in good faith, unless there is an overriding project philosophy to *contain costs*. This cost-control philosophy should be embedded in the program development methodology so that every solution is examined in search of more cost-effective answers. Assumptions and generalities must continually be challenged in light of the overwhelming interest in *low-cost* solutions.

Allocating resources to develop a contingency program is a difficult task, made even tougher by the fact that it is virtually impossible to cost-justify how much to spend. There is a big difference between conducting a risk analysis or business impact analysis and cost justification. It can be calculated with reasonable precision how much would be lost per day if a particular production line could not operate. However, because there are no reliable probability statistics on the impact of specific disasters on *business continuity,* the cost-justification calculation cannot be completed.

This difficulty is compounded by the fact that cost-conscious executives are reluctant to commit funds for a *detailed program* for an event of which the scope and dimensions are unclear, such as a sudden disaster. This is because most plans imply precise logistical and procedural commitments that translate into high maintenance costs. Given the low probability of a disaster and the high cost of redundancy, the goal following a disaster should be to stabilize operations. The real challenge lies in developing cost-effective alternate procedures to support vital business functions until normal processing capability can be restored. Loss of efficiency during a disaster recovery period should never be used to justify spending more money than necessary on alternate interim processing strategies that would be in effect for only a few days.

BACKUP

When a service fails, the primary responsibility of the provider must be *recovery.* The primary responsibility of the user is *continuity of operations.* When there is a power blackout, the consumer worries about how to get along without electricity, whereas the public utility is concerned about how to restore electricity. Similarly, data processing is responsible for a backup power supply should electricity fail. The materials department, however, is responsible for a contingency program for inventory control if the computer fails, Included in this rationale is the somewhat less obvious fact that users have far more choice and flexibility than the provider. In general, the only strategy for the provider that will serve all users is instant recovery. If that can be achieved, then, by definition, there has been no disaster. The problem is that maintaining duplicate facilities is prohibitively costly.

2

WORKPLACE VIOLENCE

BACKGROUND

What Is Workplace Violence?

Workplace violence is violent action or the threat of violent action against workers or an organization. Terrorism can be an example of workplace violence. It can occur at or outside the workplace and can range from threats and verbal abuse to physical assaults and homicide, one of the leading causes of job-related deaths. In whatever form it takes, workplace violence is a growing concern for organizations worldwide.

Who Is Vulnerable?

The Occupational Safety and Health Administration (OSHA) claims some 2 million U.S. workers are victims of workplace violence annually. It can strike anywhere and anytime, and no one or no organization is immune. Most vulnerable are workers who exchange money with the public; deliver passengers, goods, or services; or work alone or in small groups. Equally vulnerable are those who work late-night or early-morning hours; and/or work in high-crime areas, or in community settings and homes where they have extensive contact with the public.

Also prime targets are healthcare and social service workers, such as visiting nurses, psychiatric evaluators, and probation officers; community workers, such as gas and water utility employees, phone and cable TV installers, and postal workers; and retail workers.

Contributing Factors

These conditions or organizational practices contribute to the likelihood of workplace violence:

- Lack of a preventive policy toward workplace violence
- Inadequate employee acquisition, supervision, and retention practices
- Inadequate training on violence prevention
- No clearly defined rules of conduct
- Inability of supervisors to assess threats
- No mechanism for reporting individuals exhibiting behavior likely to lead to workplace violence
- Failure to take immediate action against those who have threatened or committed acts of violence

LIABILITY

Employer Liability

According to the *Employment Law Review:*

While there are no absolute predictors available to completely prevent workplace violence, employers must take proactive measures to reduce their risk of liability should an incident happen at their workplace. Several legal statutes and common law theories impose obligations on employers to provide a safe working environment. A few of the more common theories are as follows:

- *OSHA liability.* Under the Occupational Safety and Health Act ("OSHA"), employers have a duty to furnish a safe and healthful working environment for their employees. If some basis exists to suspect a problem and no action is taken, OSHA could argue that a breach of the duty to provide a safe environment has occurred. An employer who fails to comply with this duty may be fined up to $70,000 for each infraction, based on the gravity of the violation. Criminal penalties may also be imposed against individual supervisors under this federal statute. Employers should also keep in mind that many states have occupational safety and health statutes which impose a duty to provide a safe and healthful working environment. Again, monetary fines and criminal penalties may be imposed for violations.

- *Negligence.* Under the theory of negligence, employers may be liable to others when they have breached a duty to use reasonable care to prevent a foreseeable risk of injury to those parties. With regard to workplace violence, employers have a duty to provide a safe working environment; warn of dangerous conditions; hire, retain, and supervise non-violent personnel; and provide adequate security.

An employer may be held liable to employees and third parties for negligent hiring, retention, and supervision. Negligent hiring occurs when an employer knew, or should have known, of an applicant's violent propensities but hired the applicant nonetheless. To avoid such liability, employers must make adequate pre-employment background investigations.

Likewise, negligent retention and supervision focuses on whether an employer had notice that an employee posed a threat to the safety of others and failed to protect them. To protect themselves from these types of claims, employers must take proactive measures to investigate reports or observations of violent propensities and to follow through with discipline, termination, and notices to potential victims as the investigations deemed warranted.

Employers may also be held liable as landowners by failing to provide adequate security on workplace premises. As a landowner (or possessor of land), an employer is under legal duty to exercise reasonable care under the circumstances to maintain the property in a safe condition. This duty includes taking precautions to protect others from reasonably foreseeable harmful acts of a third party and to warn of known concealed dangers. This duty includes providing reasonable protection to prevent violent conduct by third parties whom the landowner knows, or should realize, are dangerous. Thus, as landowners, employers must implement adequate physical security measures (i.e., keyed entries) and warn the employees of any known dangers.[1]

Security

In 1985, the Port Authority of New York and New Jersey launched an investigation into possible workplace violence at the World Trade Centers (WTC). The report concluded:

> A time-bomb laden vehicle could be driven into the W.T.C. and parked in the public parking area. The driver would then exit via elevator into the W.T.C. and proceed with his business unnoticed. At a predetermined time, the bomb could be exploded in the basement.[2]

In 1991, a second report found that "the major risk to the Trade Center was from a package or hand-held bomb, and that the shopping and pedestrian areas, not the parking garage, would be the most likely target."[3]

Following the February 26, 1993, World Trade Center bombing, security in the public parking area and pedestrian entrances of both buildings was strengthened considerably.

Workplace Violence Incidents

Examples of the types and causes of workplace violence incidents follow.

- *September 12, 2001.* After a man made a bomb threat to his employer, a large retail chain store in Tampa, police were sent to the residence of the perpetrator to follow up the investigation. The perpetrator pulled a knife on a police officer and was shot to death.

- *September 12, 2001.* A distraught Denver Fire captain allegedly gunned down his supervisor before turning the gun on himself.

- *September 26, 2001.* At a Detroit auto parts plant, a man chased his former girlfriend through her workplace, killed her, then turned the gun on himself.

- *December 6, 2001.* An employee of a large wood products manufacturing plant in Goshen, Indiana, who was pending termination shot and killed one employee and wounded six others before committing suicide.

- *January 16, 2002.* Following academic dismissal at a Virginia law school, a former law student allegedly killed two professors and one student and wounded three others before being subdued by bystanders.

- *January 30, 2002.* At a school district bus garage in Zanesville, Ohio, a school bus driver allegedly walked into a coworker's bus and opened fire, killing her, then himself.

- *March 1, 2002.* A worker at a Silicon Valley biotech firm shot and killed his former boss and then turned the gun on himself.

- *March 22, 2002.* Fearing pending termination, a worker at an aviation parts manufacturing plant in South Bend, Indiana, shot three employees to death, wounded another four employees, and later committed suicide.

- *April 5, 2002.* At a worldwide telecommunications firm in Raleigh, North Carolina, a disgruntled employee allegedly made threats to fly his airplane into his workplace. He was fired and arrested for terrorist threats.

- *January 30, 2005.* A woman who had been placed on medical leave for psychological problems shot and killed five former colleagues and critically wounded another at a postal sorting plant in Goleta, California, before fatally shooting herself. The woman, who had not worked there for two years, drove to the plant and followed another employee closely in her car through a security gate. She then confronted another employee at gunpoint, taking an electronic identification badge to gain access to the building. There were no security guards.

Three Stages Prior to Workplace Violence

While profiling predictors of workplace violence is difficult, three consecutive phases of conduct generally precede such incidents:

1. *Disgruntlement.* An individual complains to colleagues about management/issues in general.
2. *Identifies target.* An individual names the manager or supervisor who is causing the distress.
3. *Gets ready to act.* An individual makes certain insurance premiums are paid, asks about pension payout/coverage, and takes home family photos.

PREVENTION

Policy and Strategy

Employers should create and enforce a zero-tolerance policy against workplace violence. The policy should prohibit harassment, threats of violence and intimidation, and weapon possession on premises. The policy should also assign responsibility to receive, investigate, and respond to reports of threats or conduct. It should also provide guidance in recognizing warning signs of conduct and reporting suspects, ensure workforce safety of the during a violent incident, and provide postincident counseling.

A workplace violence *policy* statement should indicate that recent terrorism and workplace violence demands a broad scope of contingency programs that protect *facilities* and include *employee-related* programs aimed at prevention.

Workplace Violence and Boards of Directors

While every employer hopes that the workplace is safe from the violent atrocities that are headlined in the media, statistics show that no place of employment is immune. In light of this reality, boards of directors should urge organizations to take proactive steps to implement policies and procedures to protect employees from harm and themselves from liability. Human resources (HR) is the most logical discipline to implement these programs.

Reducing Exposure to Workplace Violence

One way for employers to reduce exposure to workplace liability is to perform thorough prehiring investigations and background checks. By conducting complete applicant reference and background checks, employers can discern significant information and create a valid defense to a claim of negligent hiring. However, employers must balance the need to know with the applicant's right to privacy and antidiscrimination laws. The most prudent solution is to ask the applicant to sign an authorization and release form, authorizing former employers to disclose all information in their personnel files.

After employees are hired, employers should provide mandatory training on workplace violence. Supervisors should be trained to recognize the early warning signs of a potentially violent employee, to resolve disputes through effective communications, to handle terminations, and to respond to and diffuse a potentially violent incident.

By preventing unauthorized access to the workplace, employers can reduce the risk of a former employee or outsider entering the premises to commit an act of violence. A proper security plan might include keyed access, guards, and cameras.

What Can Employers Do to Protect Employees?

The best protection employers can offer is to establish a zero-tolerance policy toward workplace violence against or by their employees. The employer should establish a workplace violence prevention program or incorporate the information into an existing accident prevention program, employee handbook, or manual of standard operating procedures. It is important that employees understand that all claims of workplace violence will be investigated and remedied promptly. Employers can also:

- Instruct employees on what to do if they witness or are subject to workplace violence, and how to protect themselves.
- Install video surveillance cameras, extra lighting, and alarm systems to minimize access by outsiders.
- Provide drop safes to limit the amount of cash on hand.
- Equip field staff with cellular phones and handheld alarms or noise devices and keep a contact person informed of their location throughout the day.
- Instruct employees not to enter any location where they feel unsafe.
- Provide a 1-800 number 24 hours a day where employees, without identifying themselves, can report the names of individuals and/or conduct they think could escalate into a workplace violence incident.

How Can Employees Protect Themselves?

While nothing can guarantee an employee will not become a victim of workplace violence, these steps will reduce the odds:

- Learn how to recognize, avoid, or diffuse potentially violent situations by attending training programs.

- Alert supervision to any concerns about safety or security.
- Report any disruptive or suspect behavior immediately.
- Avoid traveling alone into unfamiliar locations.
- Carry minimal amounts of money.

Warning Signs of Violence

No one can predict human behavior and there is no specific "profile" of a potentially dangerous individual. However, indicators of increased risk of violent behavior include:

- Direct or veiled threats of harm
- Intimidating, belligerent, harassing, bullying, or other inappropriate and aggressive behavior
- Numerous conflicts with supervisors and other employees
- Bringing a weapon to the workplace, brandishing a weapon in the workplace, making inappropriate references to guns, or fascination with weapons
- Statements showing fascination with incidents of workplace violence, statements indicating approval of the use of violence to resolve a problem, or statements indicating identification with perpetrators of workplace homicides
- Statements indicating desperation (over family, financial, and other personal problems) to the point of contemplating suicide
- Drug/alcohol abuse
- Extreme changes in behaviors

Performance Indicators

Examples of work-related conduct that could well be warning signs of employee discontent and might lead to workplace violence include:

- Attendance problems
- Poor work performance

- Poor workplace relationships
- Acts of insubordination
- Blames others for difficulties
- Indications of substance abuse
- Subtle acts of intimidation
- Poor hygiene/appearance

Employee Training

Employees should know how to report incidents of violent, intimidating, threatening, and other disruptive behavior. Employees should also be provided with phone numbers for quick reference during a crisis or an emergency. Employee workplace violence prevention training should include:

- Explanation of workplace violence policy
- Encouragement to report incidents
- Ways of preventing or diffusing volatile situations or aggressive behavior
- How to deal with hostile persons
- Managing anger
- Techniques and skills to resolve conflicts
- Stress management
- Security procedures

Supervisory Training

Supervisory training should include basic leadership skills, such as setting clear standards, addressing employee problems promptly, and using the probationary period, performance counseling, discipline, and other management tools conscientiously. Supervisors do not need to be experts in violent behavior; what is needed is a willingness to seek advice from experts.

Alternate Dispute Resolution

Alternate dispute resolution (ADR) is most useful in preventing workplace violence when a problem first surfaces, that is, before an employee's conduct rises to a level that warrants disciplinary action. ADR techniques include:

- *Facilitation.* This technique is most useful when the intensity of emotions are low, there is no apparent polarization, or the parties have enough trust in each other that they can work together to develop a mutually acceptable solution.
- *Ombudsmen.* These problem-solvers use techniques including counseling, mediation, conciliating, and fact-finding to find a solution to conflict. Typically, ombudsmen interview the parties, review information and policies, and offer options to the disputants.
- *Mediation.* Mediation is useful in highly polarized disputes where the parties have been unable to initiate a productive dialogue or have been talking and have reached a seemingly insurmountable impasse.
- *Interest-based problem solving.* This method creates effective solutions while improving the relationship between the parties. The process separates the person from the problem, explores all interests to clarify issues, brainstorms solutions, and uses some mutually-agreed-on standard to reach closure.
- *Peer review.* In this problem-solving process, an employee takes a dispute to a panel of fellow employees and supervisors for a solution.

Incident Response Team Training

Incident response team training should include discussions of policy, legal constraints, and other professional concerns. Additional training can be accomplished by practicing responses to different scenarios of workplace violence. Practice exercises can help team members understand each other's responses to various situations so that there is less confusion or misunderstanding during an actual incident.

INCIDENT RESPONSE

Critical Incident Stress Debriefing

Debriefings are group meetings designed to give participants an opportunity to discuss their thoughts and feelings about a distressing event in a controlled and rational manner, and to help them understand they are not alone in their reactions. It is recommended that debriefings be held within 24 to 72 hours following an incident.

Critical incident stress debriefing (CISD) is a debriefing model designed to minimize the impact of an incident on an individual's life and assists the recovery process. It includes these phases:

- *Introductory phase* begins by the leader listing these ground rules:
  - Participation is encouraged.
  - No one is compelled to talk.
  - No notes or recordings can be made.
  - Confidentiality is maintained.
  - The process is not intended as therapy.

- *Fact phase* begins with the leader asking participants to briefly mention their degree of involvement with the incident. Participants may then begin to relate their first reactions to the incident.

- *Thought phase* asks participants to describe their first thoughts following the incident. It is a process that begins to personalize the experience.

- *Reaction phase* involves asking participants to discuss what was the worst part of the event for them personally. This phase causes participants to explore some of their deeper, personal responses to the event.

- *Symptom phase* is when participants are asked to describe any symptoms of distress: (1) at the time of the incident, (2) that arose during the next few days, and (3) that they are still experiencing.

- *Teaching phase* is the sharing of information regarding the relationship between the critical incident and the subsequent cognitive, emotional, behavioral, and psychological reactions that others involved in such events have experienced.

- *Reentry phase* signals the end of the debriefing. Participants are encouraged to ask questions and explore other issues. The leader delivers the message that the participant's reactions are a normal response to an abnormal event.

Recommendation

Despite the best-laid plans, violence in the workplace can and does happen. Prevention and training are the best approach.

Notes

[1] Lisa A. Schworm, "Workplace Violence: How Employers Can Protect Themselves While Protecting Their Employees," *Employment Law Review,* no. 3 (Reed Smith LLP), January 2000.

[2] Anemona Hartocollis, "Port Authority Held Negligent in 1993 Bombing," *New York Times,* October 27, 2005.

[3] *Ibid.*

3

FINAL REPORTS OF THE FEDERAL BUILDING AND FIRE INVESTIGATION OF THE WORLD TRADE CENTER DISASTER

INTRODUCTION

The collapse of New York City's World Trade Center (WTC) structures following the terrorist attacks of September 11, 2001, was the worst building disaster in recorded history, killing some 2,800 people. More than 350 fire and emergency responders were among those killed, the largest loss of life for this group in a single incident.

Genesis of This Investigation

Immediately following the terrorist attack on the WTC on September 11, 2001, the Federal Emergency Management Agency (FEMA) and the American Society of Civil Engineers began planning a building performance study of the disaster. The week of October 7, as soon as the rescue and search efforts ceased, the Building Performance Study Team went to the site and began its assessment. This was to be a brief effort, as the study team consisted of experts who largely volunteered their time away from their other professional commitments. The Building Performance Study issued its report in May 2002, fulfilling its goal "to determine probable failure mechanisms and to identify areas of future investigation that could lead to practical measures for improving the damage resistance of buildings against such unforeseen events."

On August 21, 2002, with funding from the U.S. Congress, the National Institute of Standards and Technology (NIST) announced its building and fire safety investigation of the WTC disaster. On October 1, 2002, the National Construction Safety Team Act was signed into law. The NIST investigation was conducted under the authority of the National Construction Safety Team Act.

The goals of the investigation of the WTC disaster were to investigate the building construction, the materials used, and the technical conditions that contributed to the outcome.

The investigation would serve as a basis for:

- Improvements in the way buildings are designed, constructed, maintained, and used
- Improved tools and guidance for industry and safety officials
- Recommended revisions to current codes, standards, and practices
- Improved public safety

The specific objectives were:

- Determine why and how WTC 1 and WTC 2 collapsed following the initial impacts of the aircraft and why and how WTC 7 collapsed
- Determine why the injuries and fatalities were so high or low depending on location, including all technical aspects of fire prevention, occupant behavior, evacuation, and emergency response
- Determine what procedures and practices were used in the design, construction, operation, and maintenance of WTCs 1, 2, and 7
- Identify, as specifically as possible, areas in current building and fire codes, standards, and practices that warrant revision

November 29, 2005 Report Recommendations

The report had 30 recommendations across seven different areas:

1. Increased structural integrity
2. Enhanced fire endurance of structures

3. New methods for fire-resistant design of structures
4. Improved active fire protection
5. Improved emergency response
6. Improved procedures and practices
7. Education and training

The following pages reflect these recommendations.

INCREASED STRUCTURAL INTEGRITY

Recommendation 1

NIST recommends that (1) progressive collapse be prevented in buildings through the development and nationwide adoption of consensus standards and code provisions, along with the tools and guidelines needed for their use in practice; and (2) a standard methodology be developed/supported by analytical design tools and practical design.

Affected Standards and Codes
AFFECTED STANDARDS
ASCE-7—AISC Specifications, and ACI 318—Building Code Requirements for Structural Concrete. These standards and other relevant committees should draw on expertise from ASCE/SFPE 29 for issues concerning progressive collapse under fire conditions.

MODEL BUILDING AND FIRE CODES
The consensus standards should be adopted in model building codes, that is, the *International Building Code* and NFPA 5000 by mandatory reference to or incorporation of, the latest edition of the standard. State and local jurisdictions should adopt and enforce the improved model building codes and national standards based on all 30 WTC recommendations. The codes and standards may vary from the WTC recommendations but satisfy their intent.

Affected Organizations
    American Concrete Institute
    American Institute of Steel Construction
    American Society of Civil Engineers
    International Code Council
    National Fire Protection Association

Recommendation 2

NIST recommends that nationally accepted performance standards be developed for (1) conducting wind tunnel testing of prototype structures based on sound technical methods that result in repeatable and reproducible results among testing laboratories; and (2) estimating wind loads and their effects on tall buildings for use in design, based on wind tunnel testing data and directional wind speed data.

Affected Standards and Codes
AFFECTED STANDARD
ASCE-7.

MODEL BUILDING AND FIRE CODES
Minimum Design Loads for Buildings and Other Structures. The standard should be adopted in model building codes by mandatory eference to, or incorporation of, the latest edition of the standard.

Affected Organization
American Society of Civil Engineers

Recommendation 3

NIST recommends that an appropriate criterion be developed and implemented to enhance the performance of tall buildings by limiting sway under lateral load design conditions, that is, winds and earthquakes.

Affected Standards and Codes
AFFECTED STANDARDS
ASCE-7 Specifications and ACI 318—Building Code Requirements for Structural Concrete.

MODEL BUILDING AND FIRE CODES
The standards should be adopted in model building codes by mandatory reference to, or incorporation of, the latest edition of the standard.

Affected Organizations
American Concrete Institute

American Institute of Steel Construction

American Society of Civil Engineers

ENHANCED FIRE ENDURANCE OF STRUCTURES

Recommendation 4

NIST recommends evaluating and, where needed, improving the technical basis for determining appropriate construction classification and fire rating requirements (especially for tall buildings)—and making related code changes now as much as possible—by explicitly considering factors including:

- Timely access by emergency responders and full evacuation of occupants, or the time required for burnout without partial collapse
- The extent to which redundancy in active fire protection (sprinkler and standpipe, fire alarm, and smoke management) systems should be credited for occupant life safety
- The need for redundancy in fire protection systems that are critical to structural integrity
- The ability of the structure and local floor systems to withstand a maximum credible fire scenario without collapse, recognizing that sprinklers could be compromised, not operational, or nonexistent
- Compartmentation requirements to protect the structure, including fire-related doors and automatic enclosures, and limiting air supply (e.g., thermally resistant window assemblies) to retard fire spread in buildings with large, open floor plans
- The effect of spaces containing unusually large fuel concentrations for the expected occupancy of the building
- The extent to which fire control systems, including suppression by automatic or manual means, should be credited as part of the prevention of fire spread

Affected Standards and Codes
MODEL BUILDING AND FIRE CODES
A comprehensive review of current construction classifications and fire rating requirements and the establishment of a uniform set of revised

thresholds with a firm technical basis that considers the factors identified above should be undertaken.

Affected Organizations

International Code Council

National Fire Protection Association

Recommendation 5

NIST recommends that the technical basis for the century-old standard for fire resistance testing of components, assemblies, and systems be improved through a national effort. Necessary guidance also should be developed for extrapolating the results of tested assemblies to prototypical building systems. A key step in fulfilling this recommendation is to establish a capability for studying and testing the components, assemblies, and systems under realistic fire and load conditions.

Affected Standards and Codes
AFFECTED STANDARDS
ASTM International, ASTM E119—Standard Test Methods for Fire Tests of Building Construction and Materials, NFPA 251—Standard Methods of Tests of Fire Endurance of Building Construction and Materials, UL 263 and ISO 834.

MODEL BUILDING AND FIRE CODES
The standards should be adopted in model building codes by mandatory reference to, or incorporation of, the latest edition of the standard.

Affected Organizations
American Society of Mechanical Engineers

International Organization for Standardization

National Fire Protection Association

Underwriters Laboratories

Recommendation 6

NIST recommends the development of criteria, test methods, and standards: (1) for the in-service performance of sprayed fire-resistive materials (SFRM, also commonly referred to as fireproofing or insulation) used to protect structural components; and (2) to ensure that these materials, as installed, conform to conditions in tests used to establish the fire resistance rating of components.

Affected Standards and Codes
MODEL BUILDING AND FIRE CODES
This approach is currently required by the *International Building Code* (*IBC*), one of the model codes, and is in the process of adoption by NFPA 5000, the other *model code*. This requirement ensures consistency in the fire protection provided to all of the structural elements that contribute to overall structural stability. State and local jurisdictions should adopt and enforce this requirement.

Affected Organizations
American Concrete Institute

American Institute of Architects

Association of the Wall and Ceiling Industry

ASTM International

Recommendation 7

NIST recommends the adoption and use of the "structural frame" approach to fire resistance ratings.

Affected Standards and Codes
MODEL BUILDING AND FIRE CODES
This approach is currently required by the *International Building Code* (*IBC*), one of the model codes, and is in the process of adoption by NFPA 5000, the other *model code.* This requirement ensures consistency in the fire protection provided to all of the structural elements that contribute to overall structural stability. State and local jurisdictions should adopt and enforce this requirement.

Affected Organizations
None.

NEW METHODS FOR FIRE-RESISTANT DESIGN OF STRUCTURES

Recommendation 8

NIST recommends that the fire resistance of structures be enhanced by requiring a performance objective that uncontrolled building fires result in burnout without partial or global (total) collapse.

Affected Standards and Codes
AFFECTED STANDARDS
ASCE-7—AISC Specifications, ACI 318—Building Code Requirements for Structural Concrete, and ASCE/SFPE 29—Standard Calculation Methods for Structural Fire Protection.

MODEL BUILDING AND FIRE CODES
This recommendation should be included into the national model codes as an objective and adopted as an integral part of fire resistance design for structures. The issue of nonoperational sprinklers could be addressed using the existing concept of Design Scenario 8 of NFPA 5000, where such compromise is assumed and the result is required to be acceptable to the Authority having juristiction.

Affected Organizations
    American Concrete Institute
    American Institute of Steel Construction
    American Society of Civil Engineers
    National Fire Protection Association
    Society of Fire Protection Engineers

Recommendation 9

NIST recommends the development of: (1) performance-based standards and code provisions, as an alternative to current prescriptive design methods, to enable the design and retrofit of structures to resist real building fire conditions, including their ability to achieve the performance objective of burnout without structural or local floor collapse; and (2) the tools, guidelines, and test methods necessary to evaluate the fire performance of the structure as a whole system.

Affected Standards and Codes
AFFECTED STANDARDS
ASCE-7—AISC Specifications, ACI 318, and ASCE/SFPE 29 for fire-resistance design and retrofit of structures; NFPA, SFPE, ASCE, and ISO TC92 SC4 for building multicompartment, multifloor design basis fire scenarios; and ASTM, NFPA, UL and ISO for new test methods.

MODEL BUILDING AND FIRE CODES
The performance standards should be adopted as an alternative method in model building codes by mandatory reference to, or incorporation of, the latest edition of the standard.

Affected Organizations
American Concrete Institute
American Steel Institute
American Society of Civil Engineers
ASTM International
International Organization for Standardization
National Fire Protection Association

Recommendation 10

NIST recommends the development and evaluation of new fire-resistive coating materials, systems, and technologies with significantly enhanced performance and durability to provide protection following major events.

Affected Standards and Codes
AFFECTED STANDARDS
Technical barriers, if any, to the introduction of new structural fire-resistance materials, systems, and technologies should be identified and eliminated in the AIA MasterSpec, AWCI Standard 12, and ASTM standards for field inspection, conformance criteria, and test methods.

MODEL BUILDING AND FIRE CODES
Technical barriers, if any, to the introduction of new structural fire-resistance materials, systems, and technologies should be eliminated from the model building codes.

Affected Organizations
ASTM International

American Institute of Architects

Association of the Wall and Ceiling Industry

Recommendation 11

NIST recommends that the performance and suitability of advanced structural steel, reinforced and prestressed concrete, and other high-performance material systems be evaluated for use under conditions expected in building fires.

Affected Standards and Codes
AFFECTED STANDARDS
AISC Specifications and ACI 318. Technical barriers, if any, to the introduction of these advanced systems should be eliminated in ASTM E 119—Standard Test Methods for Fire Tests of Building Construction and Maintenance, NFPA 251—Standard Methods of Test of Fire Endurance of Building Construction and Materials, UL 263—Fire Tests of Building Construction and Materials, ISO 834—Fire Resistance Tests.

MODEL BUILDING AND FIRE CODES
Technical barriers, if any, to the introduction of these advanced systems should be eliminated from the model building code.

Affected Organizations
American Concrete Association

ASTM International

International Organization for Standardization

National Fire Protection Association

Underwriters Laboratories

IMPROVED ACTIVE FIRE PROTECTION

Recommendation 12

NIST recommends that the performance and possibly the redundancy of active fire protection systems (sprinklers, standpipe/hoses, fire alarms, and smoke management systems) in buildings be enhanced to accommodate the greater risks associated with increasing building height and population, increased use of open spaces, high-risk building activities, fire department response limits, transient fuel loads, and higher threat profile.

Affected Standards and Codes
AFFECTED STANDARDS
NFPA 13, NFPA 14, NFPA 20, NFPA 72, NFPA 90A, NFPA 92A, NFPA 92B, and NFPA 101.

MODEL BUILDING AND FIRE CODES
The performance standards should be adopted in model building codes by mandatory reference to, or incorporation of, the latest edition of the standard.

Affected Organization
National Fire Protection Association

Recommendation 13

NIST recommends that fire alarm and communications systems in buildings be developed to provide continuous, reliable, and accurate information on the status of life safety conditions at a level of detail sufficient to manage the evacuation process in building fire emergencies; all communication and control paths in buildings need to be designed and installed to have the same resistance to failure and increased survivability above that specified in present standards.

Affected Standards and Codes
AFFECTED STANDARDS
NFPA 1—Fire Prevention Code, NFPA 72—National Fire Alarm Code, and NFPA 101—Life Safety Code.

MODEL BUILDING AND FIRE CODES
The performance standards should be adopted in model building and fire codes by mandatory reference to, or incorporation of, the latest edition of the standard.

Affected Organization
National Fire Protection Association

Recommendation 14

NIST recommends that control panels at fire/emergency command stations in buildings be adapted to accept and interpret a larger quantity of more reliable information from the active fire protection systems that provide tactical decision aids to fireground commanders, including water flow rates from pressure and flow devices, and that standards for their performance be evaluated.

Affected Standards and Codes
AFFECTED STANDARDS
NFPA 1—Fire Prevention Code, NFPA 72—National Fire Alarm Code, and NFPA 101—Life Safety Code.

MODEL BUILDING AND FIRE CODES
The performance standards should be adopted in model building and fire codes by mandatory reference to, or incorporation of, the latest edition of the standard.

Affected Organization
National Fire Protection Association

Recommendation 15

NIST recommends that systems be developed and implemented for: (1) real-time off-site secure transmission of valuable information from fire alarm and other monitored building systems for use by emergency responders, at any location, to enhance situational awareness and response decisions and maintain safe and efficient operations; and (2) preservation of that information either off-site or in a black box that will survive a fire or other building failure for purposes of subsequent investigations and analysis. Standards for the performance of such systems should be developed, and their use should be required.

Affected Standards and Codes
AFFECTED STANDARDS
NFPA 1, NFPA 72, and NFPA 101.

MODEL BUILDING AND FIRE CODES
The performance standards should be adopted in model building and fire codes by mandatory reference to, or incorporation of, the latest edition of the standard.

Affected Organization
    National Fire Protection Association

IMPROVED BUILDING EVACUATION

Recommendation 16

NIST recommends that public agencies, nonprofit organizations concerned with building and fire safety, and building owners and managers develop and carry out public education and training campaigns, jointly and on a nationwide scale, to improve building occupants' preparedness for evacuation in case of building emergencies.

Affected Standards and Codes
AFFECTED STANDARDS
UCC/ANSI A117-1.

MODEL BUILDING AND FIRE CODES
The standard should be adopted in model building and fire codes by mandatory reference to, or incorporation of, the latest edition of the standard.

Affected Organizations
American National Standards Institute
Building Owners & Managers Association
Council on Tall Buildings and Urban Habitat
National Conference of States on Building Codes & Standards
National Fire Prevention Association
National Institute of Building Sciences

Recommendation 17

NIST recommends that tall buildings be designed to accommodate timely full-building evacuation of occupants when required in building-specific or large-scale emergencies, such as widespread power outages, major earthquakes, tornados, hurricanes without sufficient advanced warning, fires, explosions, and terrorist attack.

Building size, population, function, and iconic status should be taken into account in designing the egress system. Stairwell capacity and stair discharge door width should be adequate to accommodate counterflow due to emergency access by responders.

Affected Standards and Codes
AFFECTED STANDARDS
NFPA 101—Life Safety Code, ASME A 17—Elevators and Escalators.

MODEL BUILDING AND FIRE CODES
The standard should be adopted in model building and fire codes by mandatory reference to, or incorporation of, the latest edition of the standard.

Affected Organizations
American Society of Mechanical Engineers
National Fire Protection Association

Recommendation 18

NIST recommends that egress systems be designed: (1) to maximize remoteness of egress components, that is, stairs, elevators, exits, without negatively impacting the average travel distance; (2) to maintain their functional integrity and survivability under foreseeable building-specific or large-scale emergencies; and (3) with consistent layouts, standard signage, and guidance so that systems become intuitive and obvious to building occupants during evacuations.

Affected Standards and Codes
AFFECTED STANDARD
NFPA 101.

MODEL BUILDING AND FIRE CODES
The performance standards should be adopted in model building and fire codes by mandatory reference to, or incorporation of, the latest edition of the standard.

Affected Organization
National Fire Protection Association

Recommendation 19

NIST recommends that building owners, managers, and emergency responders develop a joint plan and take steps to ensure that accurate emergency information is communicated in a timely manner to enhance the situational awareness of building occupants and emergency responders affected by an event. This should be accomplished through better coordination of information among different emergency responder groups, efficient sharing of that information among building occupants and emergency responders, more robust design of emergency public address systems, improved emergency responder communication systems, and use of the Emergency Broadcast System (now known as the Integrated Public Alert and Warning System) and Community Emergency Alert Networks.

Affected Standards and Codes
AFFECTED STANDARDS
NFPA 101 and/or a new standard.

MODEL BUILDING AND FIRE CODES
The standard should be adopted in model building and fire codes by mandatory reference to, or incorporation of, the latest edition of the standard to the extent it is within the scope of building and fire codes.

Affected Organization
National Fire Protection Association

Recommendation 20

NIST recommends that the full range of current and next-generation evacuation technologies should be evaluated for future use, including protected/hardened elevators, exterior escape devices, and stairwell descent devices, which may allow all occupants an equal opportunity for evacuation and facilitate emergency response access.

Affected Standards and Codes
AFFECTED STANDARDS
NFPA 101, ASME A 17, ASTM E 06, and ANSI A117.1.

MODEL BUILDING AND FIRE CODES
The standards should be adopted in model building and fire codes by mandatory reference to, or incorporation of, the latest edition of the standard.

Affected Organizations
American National Standards Institute

American Society of Mechanical Engineers

ASTM International

National Fire Protection Association

IMPROVED EMERGENCY RESPONSE

Recommendation 21

NIST recommends the installation of fire-protected and structurally hardened elevators to improve emergency response activities in tall buildings by providing timely emergency access to responders and allowing evacuation of mobility-impaired building occupants.

Affected Standards and Codes

AFFECTED STANDARDS

ASME A 17, ANSI 117.1, NFPA 70, NFPA 101, NFPA 1221, NFPA 1500, NFPA 1561, NFPA 1620, and NFPA 1710.

MODEL BUILDING AND FIRE CODES

The standards should be adopted in model building and fire codes by mandatory reference to, or incorporation of, the latest edition of the standard.

Affected Organizations

American National Standards Institute

American Society of Mechanical Engineers

National Fire Protection Association

Recommendation 22

NIST recommends the installation, inspection, and testing of emergency communications systems, radio communications, and associated operating protocols to ensure that the systems and protocols: (1) are effective for large-scale emergencies in buildings with challenging radio frequency propagation environments; and (2) can be used to identify, locate, and track emergency responders within indoor building environments and in the field.

Affected Standards and Codes

AFFECTED STANDARDS:

FCC, SAFECOM, NFPA Standards on Electronic Safety Equipment, NFPA 70, NFPA 297, and NFP 1221.

MODEL BUILDING AND FIRE CODES

The standards should be adopted in model building codes by mandatory reference to, or incorporation of, the latest edition of the standard.

Affected Organizations

Department of Homeland Security

National Fire Protection Association

Recommendation 23

NIST recommends the establishment and implementation of detailed procedures and methods for gathering, processing, and delivering critical information through integration of relevant voice, video, graphical, and written data to enhance the situational awareness of all emergency responders. An information intelligence sector should be established to coordinate the effort for each incident.

Standards and Codes
AFFECTED STANDARDS
National Incident Management System (NISM), NRP, SAFECOM, FCC, NFPA 1500, NFPA 1561, NFPA 1620, NFPA 1710, and NFPA 1221.

MODEL BUILDING AND FIRE CODES
The standards should be adopted in model building codes by mandatory reference to, or incorporation of, the latest edition of the standard.

Affected Organizations
Department of Homeland Security
National Fire Protection Association

Recommendation 24

NIST recommends the establishment and implementation of codes and protocols for ensuring effective and uninterrupted operation of the command and control system for large-scale building emergencies.

Affected Standards and Codes

AFFECTED STANDARDS

NIMS, NRP, SAFECOM, FCC, NFPA Standards of Electronic Safety Equipment, NFPA 1221, NFPA 1500, NFPA 1561, NFPA 1620, and NFPA 1710.

MODEL BUILDING AND FIRE CODES

The standards should be adopted in model building codes by mandatory reference to, or incorporation of, the latest edition of the standard.

Affected Organizations

Department of Homeland Security

National Fire Protection Association

IMPROVED PROCEDURES AND PRACTICES

Recommendation 25

Nongovernmental and quasi-governmental entities that own or lease buildings and are not subject to building and fire safety code requirements of any governmental jurisdiction are nevertheless concerned about the safety of the building occupants and the responding emergency personnel. NIST recommends that such entities be encouraged to provide a level of safety that equals or exceeds the level of safety that would be provided by strict compliance with the code requirements of an appropriate governmental jurisdiction. To gain broad public confidence in the safety of such buildings, NIST further recommends that as-designed and as-built safety be certified by a qualified third party, independent of the building owner(s). The process should not use self-approval for code enforcement in areas including interpretation of code provisions, design approval, product acceptance, certification of the final construction, and postoccupancy inspections over the life of the buildings.

Affected Standards and Codes

None

Affected Organizations

None

Recommendation 26

NIST recommends that state and local jurisdictions adopt and aggressively enforce available provisions in building codes to ensure that egress and sprinkler requirements are met by existing buildings. Further, occupancy requirements should be modified where needed (such as when there are assembly use spaces within an office building) to meet the requirements in model building codes.

Affected Standards and Codes
AFFECTED STANDARDS
Provisions related to egress and sprinkler requirements in existing buildings are available in such codes as the International Existing Building Code (IEBC), International Fire Code, NFPA 1, NFPA 101, and ASME A 17.3.

Affected Organizations
   American Society of Civil Engineers
   National Fire Protection Association

Recommendation 27

NIST recommends that building codes incorporate a provision that requires building owners to retain documents, including supporting calculations and test data, related to building design, construction, maintenance, and modifications over the entire life of the building.

Means should be developed for off-site storage and maintenance of the documents. In addition, NIST recommends that relevant building information be made available in suitably designed hard copy or electronic format for use by emergency responders. Such information should be easily accessible by responders during emergencies.

Affected Standards and Codes
MODEL BUILDING AND FIRE CODES
Model building codes should incorporate this recommendation. State and local jurisdictions should adopt and enforce these requirements.

Affected Organizations
None

Recommendation 28

NIST recommends that the role of the "Design Professional in Responsible Charge" be clarified to ensure that: (1) all appropriate design professionals (including, e.g., the fire protection engineer) are part of the design team providing the standard of care when designing buildings employing innovative or unusual fire safety systems; and (2) all appropriate design professionals (including, e.g., the structural engineer and the fire protection engineer) are part of the design team providing the standard of care when designing the structure to resist fires, in buildings that employ innovative or unusual structural and fire safety systems.

Affected Standards and Codes
AFFECTED STANDARDS
MODEL BUILDING AND FIRE CODES
AIA Practice Guidelines. The IBC, which already defines the "Design Professional in Responsible Charge," be clarified to address this recommendation. The NFPA 5000 should incorporate the "Design Professional in Responsible Charge" concept and address this recommendation.

Affected Organization
American Institute of Architects

EDUCATION AND TRAINING

Recommendation 29

NIST recommends that continuing education curricula be developed and programs be implemented for: (1) training fire protection engineers and architects in structural engineering principles and design; (2) training structural engineers, architects, fire protection engineers, and code enforcement officials in modern fire protection principles and technologies, including fire-resistance design of structures; and (3) training building regulatory and fire service personnel to upgrade their understanding and skills to conduct the review, inspection, and approval tasks for which they are responsible.

Affected Standards and Codes
AFFECTED STANDARDS
AIA, SFPE, ASME, AISC, ACI, and state licensing boards.

MODEL BUILDING AND FIRE CODES
Detailed criteria and requirements should be incorporated into model building codes under the topic "Design Professional in Responsible Charge."

Affected Organizations
    American Concrete Institute
    American Institute of Architects
    American Institute of Steel Construction
    American Society of Civil Engineers
    American Society of Mechanical Engineers
    Society of Fire Protection Engineers
    State Licensing Boards

Recommendation 30

NIST recommends that academic, professional short-course, and web-based training materials in the use of computational fire and dynamics and thermo-structural analysis tools be developed and delivered to strengthen the base of available technical capabilities and human resources.

Affected Standards and Codes
AFFECTED STANDARDS
AIA, SFPE, ASCE, ASME, AISC, ACI, ICC, and NFPA.

Affected Organizations
American Concrete Institute

American Institute of Architects

American Institute of Steel Construction

American Society of Civil Engineers

American Society of Mechanical Engineers

International Code Council

National Fire Protection Association

Society of Fire Protection Engineers

LOOKING FORWARD

Consistent with the new contingency program paradigm, the days are over when we can rely on history and prior occurrences to justify management policies and practices. This is particularly true when developing *Business Continuity Strategies: Protecting Against Unplanned Disasters.*

While most of NIST's WTC study recommendations focus on standards and building code changes, many concepts and practices can be immediately implemented by organizations that are designing, building or planning to move to new facilities.

All corporate presidents, boards of directors, audit committees, and senior management share the responsibility for providing assurance to stockholders and employees that there are continuing education programs and forward-looking strategies to provide business continuity in the face of an unplanned disaster. It is the responsibility of outside auditors to insist on these practices in their management letters and audit the existence and quality of education programs and forward-looking strategies to provide business continuity in the event of an unplanned disaster.

Developing contingency strategies for an undefined and improbable disaster is seldom a high priority in a business plan. That does not excuse us from exercising due diligence.

4

New Contingency Program Paradigm

BACKGROUND

Strategies versus Plans

The word *plan* should never have been associated with disaster recovery or business continuation. According to Webster, "plan" "refers to any detailed method, formulated beforehand, for doing something." This "something" is to take reasonable steps to ensure business continuity if a disaster strikes. That does not mean dotting every "i" and crossing every "t" for all combinations of possible incidents. But it does mean doing it in a cost-effective way, considering the low probability of an unplanned disaster actually happening to a specific facility. Therefore, developing strategies that give line managers the latitude to work out details as needed makes more sense than creating detailed step-by-step procedures that probably will never be used.

One of the disturbing implications with detailed disaster recovery plans is that immediately following a facility disaster, no one will do anything to help restore operations until they sit down and read the Disaster Recovery Plan Manual to determine precisely *how* it was supposed to be done. However, most organizations that survived facility disasters never had such a manual. Department mangers were capable of quickly identifying options for ensuring business continuity depending on the specific nature of the disaster. And they were capable of working out implementation details on the fly. So instead of developing detailed plans, think *strategies*.

Terrorism has ushered in a new era of security and contingency programs. As a result of terrorist activities in America, the National Institute of Standards and Technology (NIST) recommends changes in building codes and procedures that impact structural integrity, fire resistance and endurance, fire protection, building evacuation, and emergency response.

Terrorist Incidents

- February 26, 1993, in the public parking area under New York City's World Trade Center, terrorists detonated a van packed with explosives that killed 6 people and injured 1,000. On October 27, 2005, *The New York Times* reported that a Manhattan jury found that the Port Authority of New York and New Jersey had not maintained the area in "a reasonably safe condition" and that the failure was "a substantial factor" in allowing the bombing to occur.

   More than 400 plaintiffs have lawsuits pending for lost wages, damage to businesses, and pain and suffering.

- September 11, 2001, "a day that will live in infamy," as FDR said, certainly upped the ante for contingency programs around the world. It is the date when terrorists hijacked four airliners at the same time. One crashed into the New York City World Trade Center I, and moments later another crashed into the New York City World Trade Center II. A third crashed into the Pentagon in Washington, D.C. The fourth crashed before reaching its target after passengers rushed the cockpit.

- February 26, 2002, Islamic terrorists detonated a bomb blast that damaged cars and shattered windows near the Interior Ministry in downtown Rome. Days earlier police uncovered a tunnel Muslim terrorists were digging near the U.S. Embassy in Rome.

- March 11, 2004, terrorist attacks rocked Madrid, Spain, leaving 200 dead and wounding hundreds more.

Terrorism, Workplace Violence, and Boards of Directors

Contingency programs are needed to prevent and protect against the *impact* and *consequence* of an unplanned disaster, regardless of its cause. The emergence of terrorism and threat of workplace violence demands that boards of directors insist that organizations *develop* and *periodically report on* initiatives to identify and take corrective action to eliminate conditions or policies that might encourage terrorism or workplace violence, and develop preventive programs for working with employees who display symptoms consistent with profiles of workplace violence offenders.

OLD PARADIGM

Organizational Responsibility

Disaster recovery plans were prepared mostly by information systems (IS) departments because they prepared the computer recovery plan, and no one else wanted anything to do with disaster recovery planning.

Foreign Corrupt Practices Act

The Foreign Corrupt Practices Act of 1977 was the genesis of the old paradigm. As its name implies, it was enacted following disclosure that some U.S. companies had been accused of corrupt practices (paying bribes to conduct business in foreign countries). The act was written primarily to discourage this practice and established penalties for such infractions.

However, Congress, as it continues to do today, added items to the bill that had nothing to do with the title or original purpose of the act. One such section of the act contained these points:

- Before the availability of off-the-shelf specialized software at competitive prices that there is today, each company needed to develop its own software applications. Because of the huge investment companies had in the 1950s and 1960s in identifying information needs and in designing, coding, testing and debugging, implementing, and maintaining computer applications, computer programs should be treated as assets.

- It was the responsibility of corporate executives to protect those assets, and they could be liable for failing to provide such protection.

Next, auditing firms urged clients to develop *computer* disaster recovery plans. Clients then assigned responsibility for plan development to IS.

Computer disaster recovery plans were developed by *computer* people to ensure continuity of *computer operations.*

Common Mistakes

Three common contingency planning problems to protect against follow.

1. Auditors should have recommended that clients develop *business continuity strategies* (not computer disaster recovery plans) in the event computers were inoperable. This would have made user department managers responsible for business continuity.

2. Organizations *should not have ceded plan development to IS,* because IS had a conflict of interest as providers of the service involved.

3. Computer disaster recovery plan developers *did not probe deeply enough* to discover that if computer users were provided with a recent snapshot of status, most could operate for several days or weeks without computer processing. Costly computer hot-site agreements were justified based on false assumptions.

For highlights of the Foreign Corrupt Practices Act as well as its impact on business, see Exhibits 4.1 and 4.2.

Computer Oriented

Many companies, at great expense, continue to fund development, maintenance, and testing of backup computer hot sites justified on the need to recover *computer* operations within a day or two following a localized computer disaster.

These computer hot sites were justified on this misconception: Computer processing requirements during "normal operations" would be the

EXHIBIT 4.1   Highlights of Foreign Corrupt Practices Act

- Because of the large investment in computer software development, the resultant programs and related databases are considered as much an asset as buildings and equipment.
- Just as insurance policies are used to protect physical assets, reasonable steps should be taken to prevent information processing capability disasters.
- Because computerized information processing is the lifeblood of many businesses, the protection of computer processing capability is no longer the sole responsibility of the data processing manager but extends to the board of directors.
- If businesses elect not to develop a loss prevention and business continuity plan, then they should have a well-documented analysis that justifies their position in the event of legal action by stockholders.
- Directors and management can be held personally and criminally liable for damages if they knowingly neglect this exposure.

same after an unplanned disaster. This is not true. Line managers in most organizations, if pressed to do so, will document strategies they could use to operate for days or weeks without computer processing. Would it be easy? No. But could they do it? Yes. But computer disaster recovery plan developers were not inclined to press for such strategies because they were convinced that online computerized systems were indispensable even for a few days. They were during normal operations, but not following a disaster, provided users were provided a snapshot of conditions before the disaster occurred

EXHIBIT 4.2   Impact of Foreign Corrupt Practices Act

- Computer programs and computerized data are assets.
- Auditors criticized clients for lack of a *computer disaster* recovery plan. (Instead, they should have criticized the lack of a *business continuity plan.*)
- Businesses wrongly assumed that data processing should prepare the plan. (Business continuity planning is a type of long-range strategic planning and should not be delegated to the data processing department.)
- As a result, many plans focused on restoring computer operations instead of ensuring business continuity during a brief disaster recovery period.
- Unnecessary and costly backup computer hot-site agreements were negotiated as a result of misdirected plan development strategy and lack of a plan development methodology that emphasized the importance of cost-effective solutions.

Systemic Problems

Plan Development, Maintenance, and Testing Costs

Disaster recovery plans became inordinately detailed. Much of this was caused by the consulting conundrum of trying to increase revenues while billing for services on a per-diem basis. The only way to generate large consulting fees was to ramp up hours spent on an assignment. That resulted in more detail and thicker reports.

Even when plans were developed in-house, excess detail often was present because many times consultants participated in the project, or their brains were picked at the time they presented proposals.

Asking the wrong question during plan development was a root cause of falsifying user dependency on IS following a computer disaster. In plan development meetings, users were asked, "How many days without your online reports would it be before you couldn't continue to operate?"

Make believe you were the inventory control manager. You wanted to protect your rear and didn't want to imply that what IS provided wasn't needed. Your mind-set was "business as usual." So you answered the question something like this: "I could probably do without the report for one day, but after that I would be dead in the water." IS then documented a plan requirement that the inventory control system needed to be restored within 48 hours.

But if you were asked, "If IS backs up inventory status off-site daily and is able to provide a hard-copy report of inventory status (by printing it on a different computer) as of the day prior to the computer disaster, could you operate for six weeks without the computer?" The response would have been: "As long as we have a *starting point,* we could continue to operate and update inventory availability and location. It wouldn't be easy and would take a lot of clerical effort, but we could do it if we had to."

Computer Hot-Site Costs

With the exception of real-time communications providers and process-controlled production environments, most backup computer hot sites are a waste of money. For most other organizations, backup computer hot sites are not cost-effective.

When calculating computer hot-site costs, compound them over 20 years to include the impact of the low probability of a disaster happening. It is not sufficient to cite only *annual* computer hot-site costs as a percentage of budget. And don't forget to compound the cost of money over the same period of time.

NEW PARADIGM

Mind-Set

In today's world, contingency programs must be preventive and forward focused. It is no longer sufficient for Incident Recovery to be the initial chapter. It is no longer appropriate for computers to be the only issue.

Organizational Responsibility

Organizations successful in implementing cost-effective contingency programs have predominantly delegated responsibility to human resources (HR). Information systems computer disaster recovery plan budgets were transferred to HR. All contingency program expenditures were justified and administered by HR.

Terrorism

For the most part, organizations can do little to prevent terrorism caused by radicals. However, personnel policies and practices at each facility should be reviewed annually, and employee attitude surveys conducted to detect and correct personnel policies or practices that might act as a lightning rod for a terrorism.

Facility Oriented

The focus of the new paradigm is the need to maintain business continuity functions for mission-critical facilities. "Facilities" includes corporate headquarters, manufacturing plants, and distribution centers.

Workplace Violence

Chapter 2 deals in greater detail with preventing workplace violence. A forward-looking contingency program includes annual employee sessions to revalidate and/or identify conditions that could lead to or encourage workplace violence, loss of market share, or deterioration in customer service.

It is management's responsibility to:

- Develop and maintain annual programs to detect profile behavior patterns that could lead to workplace violence
- Take initiative in implementing preventive measures
- Evaluate effectiveness of preventive measures and restrategize as needed

Contingency Program Components

Facility contingency programs have three components:

1. Prevention
2. Incident recovery
3. Interim processing

Prevention

Prevention includes awareness education and program evaluation; maintenance; and threat detection and communication.

Awareness education and program evaluation includes annual education and awareness presentations for management and employees to reaffirm the need for a contingency program. It should include small-group brainstorming sessions to identify new threats that need to be added to the program. Annual evaluation of the effectiveness of the prevention component of the program is also important. As time passes and conditions change, parts of any program can become obsolete or unimportant, and as a result, the entire program is less effective. Scheduling an annual review of a contingency program ensures a process of review and restrategizing as needed.

Maintenance consists of keeping contingency program documentation current. The most important issue is to meet annually with department managers to revalidate interim processing strategies for business functions under their responsibility.

Threat detection and communication is an ongoing process designed to:

- Identify and correct conditions or policies that are breeding discontent and could lead to workplace violence
- Identify employees who are exhibiting extreme dissatisfaction with management or management practices that, if left unchecked, could lead to workplace violence
- Implement proactive programs to work with these employees to reduce or eliminate discontent

Incident Recovery

Incident recovery includes first responders' role, start-up, and interim processing strategies approval.

First responders' role includes activities that happen automatically when an incident is reported. Police and firefighters appear and deal with their responsibilities. Ambulances appear and take injured personnel to the hospital. And hospitals notify next of kin of injuries and/or death. Because these actions are automatic, there is no need to deal with them in a contingency program.

Start-up consists of a checklist of items not to be overlooked in the flurry of activities immediately following a facility disaster. No further detail is required. Start-up items to be included are:

- Implement facility security
- Notify employees
- Notify customers
- Notify senior management
- Designate a media contact
- Maintain a log of events/decisions

Interim processing strategies approval consists of a meeting of senior executives and operating management to formally approve how the organization will service customers until normal operations can be resumed. Interim processing strategies are a collection of options that could be used to operate different departments depending on the nature of the disaster and amount of damage. These operating options were developed, documented, and revalidated annually by department mangers. IS strategy for replacing computer hardware will also be approved.

Interim Processing

Interim processing is the time between after a facility disaster has occurred and when normal operations are resumed. This period may be only hours or several months, depending on the severity of the incident. It is when interim processing strategies—*alternate ways of operating*—are put to use.

TRANSITIONING TO THE NEW PARADIGM

Organizational Responsibility

Human resources is the discipline that has been most successful in developing and administering contingency programs. HR provides an independent perspective that facilitates a balance between technology providers (IS) and production cost centers. HR also provides a corporate perspective, that is, a balance between tendencies to justify costly solutions against the low probability that disaster will occur at a specific facility.

Overall responsibility for existing and "to be developed" computer disaster recovery plans should be assigned to HR. While HR will look to IS for technical advice, overall responsibility for all facets of a contingency program should belong to HR.

Policy and Strategy

A contingency program *policy* statement should indicate that recent terrorism and workplace violence demands a broader scope of contingency programs that protect *facilities* and include *employee-related* programs aimed at prevention. Therefore, total responsibility for contingency programs is assigned to HR.

A contingency program *strategy* statement should indicate that HR will:

- Develop contingency programs for an unplanned disaster for all functions at each facility
- Develop and implement employee-related programs and recommend corporate policy changes aimed at preventing workplace violence and terrorism
- Cost-justify computer disaster recovery plans that involve the use of backup computer hot sites, warm sites, cold sites, or any other service that requires significant and/or continuing annual expenditures

Development of Interim Processing Strategies

Loss of Facilities or Production Equipment

A facilitator intimately familiar with the operating functions, as well as the implications and ramifications of various options considered, is needed to work with department/functional managers in developing interim processing strategies. The facilitator's job is to probe, challenge, and explore alternate solutions, stressing that a loss of efficiency is not justification for more costly solutions and pressing for the lowest-cost solutions.

Loss of Computer Processing

Developing interim processing strategies for the loss of computer processing with department/functional managers' requires a different approach.

Before meeting with department/functional managers, the facilitator should establish how many weeks it would take under emergency conditions to replace computer hardware. The answer is usually two to six weeks.

The facilitator controls the response and options to be considered by department/functional managers by the way the problem is framed. One should never ask an inventory control person "How many days could you function without the computer?" The answer will be something like "two days max."

The facilitator says "thanks" and goes on to the next meeting; the manager is glad the meeting wasn't lengthy and returns to more productive work.

The question asked of the department/functional manager should have been "How *could* we continue to operate for a period of six weeks if we had a computer disaster?

5

DEVELOPING A CONTINGENCY PROGRAM

MANAGEMENT'S RESPONSIBILITY

If economics is the "dismal science," then contingency planning must be "abysmal science." No one likes to look into the abyss. But given the critical dependence of businesses on technology, facilities, and specialized processes, contingency programs are a rising priority on the agenda of senior management.

Who should develop the program? Who can ensure that the program is actually workable? The most serious mistake is to have a program that exists only on paper, without the understanding or support of line managers who would have to use it to stabilize operations following a disaster. The most costly mistake is to have a program aimed at keeping computers running instead of keeping the *business* running. The most common mistake is a program that focuses on computer disasters but ignores potential physical disasters that can render vital buildings inaccessible or critical operations inoperable.

HOW MUCH MARKET SHARE COULD COST YOU?

A disaster could happen to you, for whatever reason—fire, explosion, sabotage by a disgruntled employee or former employee.

- A vital office building is severely damaged or destroyed, and restoring computer operations will take longer than hoped for. Where will administrative personnel be relocated? What is the minimum number of personnel (you certainly do not need 100 percent of normal staff) for which space is required during a "stabilization period"—how many could temporarily work from home? What backup strategy is there for entering and handling customer orders? How is everyone going to be paid on Friday? The answer is to develop and document flexible *interim processing strategies* that can be used to stabilize operations until operations return to normal.

- A critical production operation or distribution facility is severely damaged. What alternatives exist to continue production? What locations are most viable? How will you track inventory and production? How will you operate distribution centers? Perhaps most important, in a crisis of this magnitude, can you continue to service customers and maintain market share? The answer is to develop and document interim processing strategies to ensure continuity in production and distribution until operations return to normal.

PROTECT AGAINST WHAT?

For many years, the only concern for contingency planning seemed to be the temporary loss of data processing capability because that was the area first targeted by outside auditors. In fact, the real threat to business continuity is in the loss of vital buildings or critical production or distribution operations resulting from natural causes, sabotage, or environmental conditions. Outside auditors and internal auditors are pressing management to extend their contingency programs for computers to include protection against the temporary loss of access to buildings. The problem is that the mind-set, policy and strategy, and approach that were successful in addressing contingency planning for data processing are not appropriate for facility contingency planning.

Facility contingency planning is an exercise in long-range strategic planning and, as such, should be conducted by a "neutral" facilitator, not someone in a line organization or information systems staff. The detailed specifications and procedures required to back up and restore computer data are not needed to ensure business continuity in operating departments. It is difficult to keep information systems personnel from unconsciously gravitating to more and more detail because that is the way computer systems are designed. Information systems should be responsible for identifying data processing restoration strategy; a staff planner or outside facilitator should be responsible for developing facility contingency programs.

Mind-set is also different between protecting computer processing and protecting against loss of facilities. If computer equipment is damaged or destroyed, restoring operations requires precise, systematic, tightly controlled, and disciplined detailed procedures. The solutions are technical and highly structured; there are few options. This is not true for administrative departments or manufacturing operations or distribution activities. In administrative departments and production operations, there can be several different options that might be used to ensure business continuity, depending on the nature of the physical disaster, the amount of damage, and the prognosis for reentering the building. Implementation of specific actions should be left to the judgment of department managers to decide at the time a disaster actually occurs.

In addition, senior management intuitively understands that a detailed plan covering multiple combinations of types of disaster just does not make sense. They understand that highly skilled individuals head up key departments and that those individuals do not need detailed instructions on *how* to carry out their responsibilities; they only need to agree on strategies.

CONTINGENCY PLANNING REQUIRES SPECIALIZATION

In determining who might develop a program, be leery of turning the assignment over to a consulting firm that offers a broad range of services. There can be several problems. Consulting firms shuffle staff between assignments, many times without much hands-on experience in contingency planning; this can result in confusion, false starts, time delays, and excessive costs. They usually charge per diem fees (which are counterproductive), tie up key personnel in lengthy meetings, encourage unnecessarily lengthy "weigh it by the pound" reports, and produce "politically correct" reports, all of which drive up contingency program costs unnecessarily. Most consulting firms are trained in a problem-solving process that emphasizes detail, detail, and more detail—exactly the opposite of "what if" strategies that are the key to cost-effective contingency programs.

INCREASED TECHNOLOGY DEPENDENCY

Today's children are more comfortable with automation and computer technology than their parents are. Is it any wonder that a "generation gap" is a constant in dealing with computers? In but a short time, data processing has advanced from electronic accounting machines, for which each individual step of logic had to be programmed by connecting a wire from one "hub" to another, to technology enabling computers to speak and understand verbal expressions.

In the business world, computer technology has skyrocketed from tabulating historical accounting transactions to the real-time assimilation of complex analog and digital data and the formulation and execution of process control procedures with unheralded quality assurance. Computers have the capability to consistently assimilate variable data, to develop solutions, and to apply that capability to a multitude of business problems.

If we are not careful, this will lead us to a conclusion that *all* computer systems are indispensable, even for short periods of time. Nothing could be further from the truth. Although computerized "process control" systems may be indispensable in specific production environments, most management information systems are not.

For instance, most people assume that airlines are so dependent on computer systems, particularly passenger reservation systems, that they have already arranged for off-site redundant processing capability in the event of a disaster. Most major airlines do not have off-site redundant computer processing capability, and their most critical system is not passenger reservations but *airplane maintenance.*

Management rejects redundant off-site processing capability because of its cost. Management is also confident that computer processing capability will be restored before it causes significant *long-term* loss of market share.

Why are businesses convinced that computerized management information systems are indispensable, even for short periods of time? For most organizations, computer dependency during a disaster recovery period is a myth precipitated by these factors:

- Absence of a focused awareness and education program
- Failure to explore alternatives

An educational process and the exploration of viable alternatives with the right people are the key to cost-effective contingency programs.

CORPORATE ISSUE

Because disaster recovery and business continuity planning involves long-range planning considerations, it must support the business plan. There are generally three areas of exposure to be addressed:

1. Loss of communications
2. Loss of computer processing capability
3. Loss of access to facilities

Although administrative responsibility for functional areas may be controlled by individual departments, contingency planning must be centrally coordinated. Interdepartmental interfaces, dependency of one system on others, and the need to reduce duplicate planning point to the need for a well-coordinated corporatewide contingency planning process.

CONTINGENCY PROGRAM PHASES

In deciding what should be included in a contingency program, it is helpful to understand the different phases of a contingency program. A contingency program consists of 3 time periods. A complete disaster life cycle consists of four time periods (see Exhibit 5.1):

1. Prevention
2. Incident recovery
3. Interim processing

Long-range restoration strategy will depend on the specific nature of the disaster that occurred, damage assessment, and prognosis for reentering the building. You might be back in the building in four weeks or you might need to construct a whole new facility. So until a specific disaster happens, it does not make much sense to try to anticipate where, when, or how you will resume normal operations. That will be decided later by senior management, and a statement to that effect should be part of the corporate contingency planning policy and strategy.

EXHIBIT 5.1   Contingency Program Phases

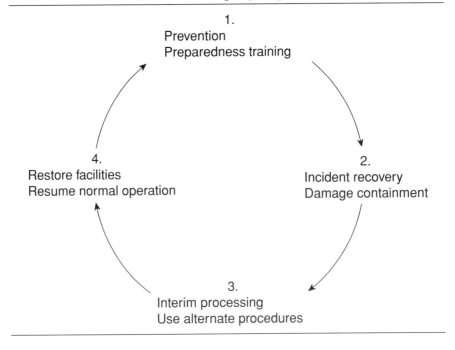

Prevention

Because most organizations will never experience a serious facility disaster, prevention is the only part of a program that will ever be used; there will never be an opportunity actually to exercise incident response nor will there be a need to call business continuity strategies into service. However, a sound prevention program is indeed important because it consists of ongoing activities that help prevent the likelihood of a disaster, such as sound physical security measures, and minimizes impact of a disaster, such as storing duplicate computer records off-site so that they can be recovered. Prevention programs should be institutionalized, that is, key responsibilities should be integrated into job descriptions and included in annual performance evaluations. A prevention program consists of all activities and responsibilities, the purpose of which is to reduce the likelihood of a disaster either to a building or to the business functions located in that building.

A prevention program is *procedural* in format because its purpose is to document ongoing responsibilities.

Incident Recovery

An incident response plan is called into action only at the time a physical disaster occurs and covers the first 24 to 48 hours following a disaster. For purposes of this book, it includes primarily issues that demand immediate attention and/or are prerequisites to maintaining business continuity; however, it does not include strategies for maintaining business continuity during a *stabilization period* as they appear in the Interim Processing section.

The most essential issues to be included in an incident recovery plan are:

- Notification to employees and customers
- Damage assessment
- Rerouting incoming phone calls and/or messaging
- Initiating restoring computer processing capability

- Physical security
- Relocating personnel

Detailed commentary about treating injuries, healthcare procedures, or other services normally provided by government or municipal agencies, departments, or institutions, are not recommended for inclusion in an incident recovery plan. It should be assumed that these agencies, departments, and institutions will perform as expected, although not as quickly in a regional disaster.

An incident recovery plan has a *checklist* format because it consists of issues that should not be overlooked in the excitement and trauma immediately following a physical disaster.

Interim Processing

Interim processing strategies are pivotal "what if" strategies for maintaining business continuity following a disaster and are developed through highly structured discussions with department line managers and key supervisors. If they are not developed with the right mind-set and expectations, are not facilitated by an individual experienced in synergistic problem solving, and do not focus exclusively on basic business functions (not computer systems), they will be part of the problem instead of part of the solution. In a worst-case scenario, one in which a building is assumed inaccessible for as long as six weeks and computer processing may not be restored for up to ten working days, two strategies need to be addressed:

1. What actions will be taken to perform tasks, such as processing customer orders and maintaining inventory status, until computer processing capability is restored?
2. What actions will be taken to stabilize operations, such as servicing customers and maintaining market share, until operations return to normal?

Developing practical interim processing strategies with line managers is where many otherwise sound plans have foundered. It involves the sensitive encounter of first-line managers and supervisors. Discomfort, insecurity, and even fear are mixed in with their logical and professional responses. If these factors are not acutely understood and carefully dealt with, they can quickly harden into resistance or evasion.

Specialists facilitating development of these "what if" strategies must respect the department managers as well as the delicate structure of an organization's policy. Only then will department managers perceive that their opinions count. It is the one part of developing a contingency program that it is worth the expense of using a specialist skilled in this highly sensitive process because it involves a different mind-set and a unique problem-solving technique.

Interim processing strategies are documented as *guidelines* because they represent options only. Department managers will determine precisely how they will proceed based on the nature of a specific incident combined with an assessment of damage.

DISCRETIONARY EXPENSE

When the economic climate is favorable, contingency planning is last on the list of things to do; when profits are down, contingency planning is the first item to be cut from the budget. Like elective surgery, contingency planning is a discretionary expense. This means that the more costly a contingency planning project is, the more likely it is that it will be repeatedly deferred.

Given that contingency planning is a discretionary cost-sensitive issue, there are two areas on which to focus in such planning:

1. Keep costs at a minimum by using a contingency program development methodology designed to yield cost-effective solutions.
2. Minimize testing requirements by encouraging "plain-vanilla" business continuity solutions that, because of their simplicity, require less exotic testing procedures.

For a representation of Contingency Program building blocks, see Exhibit 5.2.

EXHIBIT 5.2   Contingency Program Building Blocks

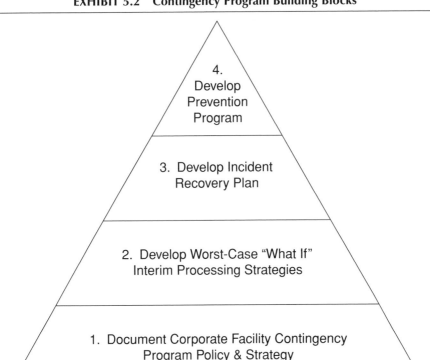

4.
Develop
Prevention
Program

3. Develop Incident
Recovery Plan

2. Develop Worst-Case "What If"
Interim Processing Strategies

1. Document Corporate Facility Contingency
Program Policy & Strategy

PROJECT PLANNING

Policy and Strategy

In developing a contingency program, there are a few problems that will be encountered. The first is that contingency planning means different things to different people, and it will be impossible to satisfy all of them. The second problem is considerable disagreement as to which items should be included in a contingency program. Compounding the first two issues is that there is little agreement on the degree of detail that a program should include. This is almost a no-win situation unless you tackle the project with a well-thought-out strategy and methodology.

Limit Scope

Which Types of Disasters?

Is the intent to include in the program all types of unplanned interruptions, regardless of how long recovery is expected to take or the significance of its impact on vital business functions? Should there be an individual scenario for each different type of disaster? Who should be responsible for declaring a disaster?

The first suggestion is to define *disaster* in terms of your own business environment. What is a disaster to a commercial bank may be only a minor disruption to a company that makes soup. It is important to structure a definition so that everyone understands, at least conceptually, what the ground rules are. Predictable incidents that cause minor inconveniences, and/or those that can be corrected in a short period of time, should not be included in a program, but should be addressed in standard operating procedures. These include incidents such as hardware component failures that are expected to be corrected within 24 hours and most software malfunctions. Programs should deal exclusively with unpredictable disasters that could result in a long-term disruption of operations.

In structuring a definition, it is well to include a time parameter that can be used as a point of reference. One organization described a disaster as (1) an unplanned incident, (2) which results in a disruption of normal operations and is expected to last longer than three working days, and (3) could have a significant impact on maintaining market share, cash flow, or servicing customers. Make certain that the definition is reasonable and appropriate for the particular business environment.

How Wide an Area?

Another question that frequently comes up is: "What about a global or regional disaster—what should the scope of our program be?" Again, the issue is what is reasonable. As the focus moves from local to regional to global disasters, the probability of occurrence diminishes. Moreover, for many organizations, it does not make any difference whether the incident is local, regional, or global, because they have only one location. If you have only one location, concentrate on maintaining business continuity with the assumption that following the disaster, there will be qualified individuals available to perform vital business functions.

For a business with multiple locations, each facility should have its own program that addresses localized outages without concern for simultaneous outages at other facilities. Keep the program flexible and avoid identifying specific alternate locations for business continuity requirements. Although it is acceptable to indicate a *first-choice* backup facility, it is not advisable to lock in a single solution without recourse.

Individual Business Units

Contingency program policy will vary among different business units because they make different products, service different markets, have different operating logistics, and may operate under different rules. Therefore, it makes sense to develop policy and strategy positions at the business-unit level. It is appropriate, however, for corporate management to insist that each business unit develop its own policy and strategy and, as a minimum, to develop interim processing strategies documenting how vital business functions would survive a disaster.

Limit the Time Periods

The biggest problem with disaster recovery programs that never seem to be completed is including too many time periods. The time periods covered should include: (1) before a disaster, (2) immediately following a disaster, and (3) stabilization.

Before a disaster is the only time period most organizations will experience because they will never have a disaster. It is the period that deals with ongoing procedures and practices that tend to reduce the likelihood of a disaster, such as physical security measures that limit access to vital buildings or critical areas. It also deals with procedures that would limit the impact of a disaster, such as storing backup copies of computer records off-site. These time period issues are usually covered in a prevention program and should be included in any contingency program.

Immediately following a disaster is a time period that normally covers the first 24 to 48 hours immediately following a facility disaster. It represents a checklist of "don't forget to do," such as notification, media management, rerouting incoming phone calls, restoring computer processing, and relocating personnel. It also includes actions that should be considered but might not have to be done, depending on the amount of damage, such as establishing a command center at another location.

Stabilization is a time period that starts about the same time as that covered by emergency response but extends for several weeks and focuses solely on stabilizing operations and maintaining business continuity until long-range restoration plans can be made. It contains business continuity strategies for all business functions aimed at protecting market share, servicing customers, and maintaining cash flow. These time period guidelines are normally covered in interim processing strategies and should be included in any contingency program. This should be the final time period included.

Restoring normal operations deserves no more than a statement explaining why it has been excluded. Determining precisely when, where, and how normal operations will be resumed will depend on several considerations: What type of disaster occurred? How much damage was actually done? What is the prognosis for reentering the building? Do we have to build a new facility? Only after damage assessment has been assimilated can these decisions be made and a *restoration strategy* approved by senior management. Therefore, a facility contingency program ends with the interim processing strategies intended for use during a stabilization period. Plans for restoring operations to normal will be developed and approved by senior management after a specific disaster has occurred.

Surgical Process

Initial meetings with department managers for the purpose of developing interim processing strategies should be brief, no more than 30 minutes long. Follow-up meetings (one should be sufficient) last no longer than 10 minutes. The review meeting lasts no more than 10 minutes. This means that a department manager is obligated to spend only a maximum of 50 minutes over a period of 30 days.

There are several important "to dos" to keep meetings brief.

First, control the conversation, where it is and where it is going. This is done by immediately—but with respect to the department manager—insisting that you are not interested in descriptions on how the department runs, or why what they do is important, but are concerned only about operating immediately following a disaster. If you do not control the conversation, you will find yourself listening to irrelevant discussions and wasting valuable time.

Second, be sure department managers understand that in formulating interim processing strategies for use during a stabilization period immediately following a facility disaster, the mind-set should be one of survival "by hook or crook," not business as usual. Explain that inefficiencies and delays are expected, some items may fall through the cracks, and there may be a temporary loss of market share. The objectives are to maintain business continuity and prevent a facility disaster from causing a significant long-term loss of market share.

Third, give department managers time parameters within which to formulate interim processing strategies for the business functions for which their department is responsible. For example, do not say, "We need to know how many days you could operate without the computer." The department manager will tell you they "couldn't possibly operate more than two days without the computer." That is the wrong question and the wrong answer. The more correct line of discussion is "We expect computer processing capability to be restored within 10 working days and need to know how you could operate without the computer for that length of time." The department manager will, in most cases, willingly explain how that can be accomplished. Asking the wrong question or asking it in the wrong context can result in causing a program that should have been completed in 30 days taking several months or years to complete. That is why it is usually cost-effective to have a skilled professional develop the initial department interim processing strategies. In following years, these strategies can be maintained with in-house personnel.

Game Plan

In determining how to go about developing a contingency program, it is important to remember two things: First, senior management is more comfortable discussing problem-solving strategies and methodologies than in participating in a problem-solving process, and, second, if you ask the wrong people (senior management) the wrong question (what is critical?), the probability is high that the quality of interim processing guidelines will be significantly compromised. The game plan should be:

- Establish contingency program policy and strategy.
- Select a program development methodology.
- Communicate policy, strategy, and methodology to senior management.
- Develop "what if" interim processing strategies with functional managers.

See Exhibit 5.3 for a sequenced list of the major steps involved in program development.

Establish a Corporate Contingency Program Policy and Strategy

Four key issues should bear heavily on program development strategy:

1. There is an extremely low probability of a disaster's happening.
2. Business continuity is the objective.
3. Loss of efficiency is expected during a stabilization period.
4. Functional department managers and supervisors must be the architects of business continuity strategies.

EXHIBIT 5.3   Major Steps in Program Development

- Develop business unit policy and strategy.
- Communicate policy, strategy, and program development methodology to senior management.
- Conduct orientation sessions.
- Develop interim processing strategies.
- Obtain functional manager approval.
- Document and publish.
- Present to senior management.

The majority of contingency planning problems, delays, and false starts can be directly attributed to failing to document a corporate contingency program policy and strategy before the planning process is initiated. If properly constructed, a corporate contingency program policy and strategy will:

- Contain program development costs.
- Reduce program maintenance and testing costs.
- Reduce the number of issues to be addressed.
- Clarify program expectations.
- Ensure a practical approach.
- Focus on strategies instead of detail.

Because it is impractical to anticipate and procedurize specific responses to an infinite number of facility disaster scenarios, corporate policy should be to immediately stabilize operations with a reduced workforce at an alternate location following a facility disaster. For planning purposes, it is anticipated a stabilization period could last six weeks.

Immediately following a facility disaster, a damage assessment team will evaluate the situation and recommend a long-range strategy for restoring normal operations. This recommendation will be based on: (1) the nature of the disaster, (2) damage assessment, and (3) the prognosis for reentering the damaged facility. During this stabilization period, senior management will approve a specific restoration plan of when, how, and where normal operations will be restored.

These factors usually apply:

- Institutionalize ongoing facility prevention programs that reduce the likelihood of facility disasters and minimize impact if one does occur.
- Maintain facility incident recovery programs that ensure an organized response to a disaster and document strategies for rerouting incoming telephone calls and restoring computer processing capability.
- Maintain relocation strategies and minimum staff requirements for use in assigning personnel to temporary facilities during a stabilization period.

- Maintain interim processing strategies that, in the absence of other instructions, can be used to service customers during a stabilization period.
- Conduct compliance audits and preparedness evaluations to ensure the continued viability of a program.

Assumptions, such as the ones that follow, should be included with a corporate policy and strategy statement to prevent getting bogged down in never-ending "what if" issues:

- A building evacuation plan exists.
- Qualified individuals will be available to execute the program.
- Incoming telephone calls will be rerouted to another facility within two hours.
- Computer processing will be restored within 10 working days.
- If relocating personnel to another company facility is required, staff at the receiving facility will be reduced to permit temporary consolidation of personnel. Personnel unable to be accommodated will work out of their residences until office space becomes available.
- Inefficiencies are expected.

See Exhibit 5.4 for a list of issues that should be included in developing policy and strategy statements for a specific business unit.

EXHIBIT 5.4 Policy and Strategy Issues

- Low probability—Explain that it is extremely unlikely that a localized disaster will occur.
- Business continuity—Emphasize the need to survive.
- Loss of efficiency—Acknowledge that inefficiency is expected and should not be used as an argument for spending money on more sophisticated solutions.
- Functional managers are architects—Explain that business continuity is a functional responsibility.
- The program is a guideline—Not expected to be read word for word, as specific actions will depend on the nature of a given disaster and the prognosis for recovery.

Select a Program Development Methodology

To understand why selection of a program development methodology is important, it is necessary to differentiate between "mechanics" (what is done) and "method" (how it is done). *Mechanics* implies precise steps to be followed. Mechanics is the rote application of programmed machine-type operations. The dictionary describes *method* as "a manner of proceeding, a technique." The distinction between these terms is great, and the penalty of acquiring a mechanical program, instead of a sound technique, is a program without substance.

BENEFITS OF A GOOD METHODOLOGY

Development of a contingency program, particularly as a contingency against a computer disaster, is not a technical issue; it is a "people problem." *The entire program development process is subjective.* The lack of credible probability statistics concerning the impact on business continuity of computer disasters makes it impossible to cost-justify how much to spend. You can theorize about how much revenue an organization might lose over a certain period of time, but you cannot arrive at a meaningful amount because of the lack of credible probability statistics. Attempting to find out what is really critical is difficult, because many department managers are reluctant to admit to a noncritical role under any circumstances. Asking "How long can you do without?" elicits a subjective answer. All through the program development process, you will be dealing not with facts but with egos and personalities. Your demeanor in addressing others is crucial; the context in which you explain the purpose of the project is important. Your conflict resolution skills will be continually challenged. Most of all, you need to have good teaching techniques to educate and continually remind program development participants about the low probability of a disaster, the high cost of redundant processing capability, and the need to look for cost-effective solutions.

The final reason that methodology is the key is that most of the people you will be working with in program development are not interested in contingency planning. They have more pressing priorities, and they cannot wait until you leave so they can get some real work done.

With considerable experience in systems and procedures, good verbal and written communications skills, and proficiency in the proper synergistic contingency planning process, a prototype program can be completed within 30 days. The prototype program can be modified further if needed, but at least it will document a solid management policy and strategy for contingencies and solutions for business continuity endorsed by department managers. Additional detail is easily added, and the prototype program can also be used as a template for other locations.

WHAT TO LOOK FOR

A sound program development methodology will (1) contain an education and awareness module, (2) address business continuity issues *before* any work is done on restoring computer operations, (3) focus on business continuity rather than technology recovery, (4) include a conflict resolution process, (5) insist that functional departments be the architects of the program, and (6) avoid unnecessary detail. See Exhibit 5.5 for a description of the major components of a sound program development methodology.

A PROBLEM-SOLVING PROCESS

Business continuity planning, a type of long-range planning, works best when orchestrated by a skilled professional using a structured problem-solving process. This process should encourage positive thinking and disallow rejection or negative opinions. By eliminating negative responses, which are a part of many group meetings, energy is focused on building solutions together, and the dynamics of that process is exciting.

EXHIBIT 5.5   Characteristics of a Good Program Development Methodology

- Begins with awareness and education program
- Awareness and education continues throughout the process
- Establishes a recovery "window" before discussions with department managers
- Emphasizes the importance of arriving at the most cost-effective solutions, considering the low probability and the long-term cost of redundant processing capability

---

PRIORITIZATION

A sound methodology will provide a basis to limit scope and thereby improve the likelihood of success. Contingency planning is a broad subject that can mean different things to different people. Some stratification or prioritization of goals is necessary. Because there are limited resources available for this type of project, there is a risk of spreading these resources so thin that their overall effect is diluted. It is more realistic to single out vital issues, such as maintaining cash flow and ensuring customer service during a stabilization period, and do them well. Most other concerns can be dealt with at a different level.

Communicate Corporate Contingency Program and Strategy

We can get into more trouble than we think by asking the wrong question of the wrong people. Contingency planning is no exception. To begin with, executives do not particularly like being asked questions by their subordinates, especially questions about issues that are removed from the mainstream of earnings per share. Instead, they expect you to bring problems to them and, at the same time, recommend one or more solutions they can examine to complete the decision-making process.

First, develop a problem statement that describes the exposure and, at the same time, recommends a strategy for addressing it. Managers are not familiar with contingency planning, and your job is to make them aware of its importance and to educate them concerning a program development process. Managers need to understand the low probability issue and the extremely high costs of providing redundancy. They also need to know that although less efficient and unpopular, there are alternate ways of surviving a disaster recovery period that should be considered.

Finally, make management comfortable with your proposed strategy by explaining that you intend to concentrate on maintaining cash flow and making certain that the organization will be able to service its customers during a stabilization period. They will like your project strategy, because you have assured them you are going to concentrate on important issues.

After getting senior management committed to a project strategy, the next job is to sell managers on a project methodology. This is not as important as selling them on project strategy, but if managers are comfortable with what you intend to do (strategy), they will feel even more comfortable if they have confidence in how you intend to accomplish it (methodology). They will also know you understand that functional division and department managers have primary responsibility for contingency planning, that you intend to work through them using a methodology that will not be disruptive to the primary mission of their department, and that you will publish a contingency program that is concise, easy to understand, and inexpensive to maintain.

Develop Business Continuity Strategies
The development of sound, well-thought-out business continuity strategies is without question the most important part of developing a contingency program. It is also the key to acceptance by both line managers and data processing personnel. More important, it is an iterative process that increasingly calls on your skills to do three things well:

1. *Position* your thinking so you can visualize the concerns of individuals; take the time to listen carefully to their concerns and suggestions.

2. *Anticipate* what the problem areas might be and then formulate conceptually what options might be available as solutions.

3. *Communicate* with other knowledgeable individuals to explore the various options and to help you begin to formulate the business continuity strategies that will be most acceptable and cost-effective.

Team Concept

There is nothing wrong with establishing different task forces to deal with specific issues during program development. However, the use of teams in carrying out the actual program should be approached with caution.

I have witnessed organizations frittering away man-hours evaluating, discussing, and debating the use of teams in program development. I have seen programs that identified no less that 16 different teams, all with specific names, addresses, e-mail addresses, phone numbers, and cell phone numbers, and with notification responsibilities. This seems like overkill by someone who has taken the team concept further than is reasonable. It is perfectly acceptable to assign responsibilities to a specific individual without any formal team. If that person is not available, then normal organizational default would apply. The important issue is to assign responsibilities to individuals, not committees or teams.

Just as big is not always better, the involvement of more people or teams of people does not necessarily improve the quality of solutions. The first principle is to assign responsibilities to specific individuals, not to a team. A contingency program covers three time periods:

1. Prevention (the period prior to the occurrence of a disaster)
2. Incident recovery (the hours immediately following a disaster)
3. Interim processing (the time when "what if" business continuity strategies will be used to support essential business functions)

Incident recovery is the only time period in which using teams should be considered, and only on an ad hoc basis. For the incident recovery period, in addition to assigning responsibilities to specific individuals, it is acceptable to identify a team of key individuals with specialized skills. It is best, however, that this team serve at the discretion of a responsible executive rather than having specific responsibilities assigned to it. Exhibit 5.6 shows the various types of teams that can be formed.

EXHIBIT 5.6   Areas in Which Teams May Be Helpful

- Administration
- Logistics
- Damage assessment
- System software
- Production control
- Computer applications
- Communications
- Computer hardware
- Facilities
- Resumption

Organization Chart

Even if you are in an environment in which you know reporting relationships, ask for a formal organization chart. You may find some surprises. You may decide in some instances to go around the formal organization to get the job done. Make certain that you have a copy of the formal organization to refer to, remembering that one of the quickest ways to damage a project is to irritate or upset key players by not being considerate of reporting relationships. Thoughtfulness, consideration, and courtesy can make up for a world of technical mistakes.

Telephone Directory

Do not start a project without an organization telephone directory. You will continually be given names of individuals to contact for various reasons. A company telephone directory will eliminate the need to ask for telephone numbers and thereby increase productivity and help to make certain that you do not misspell names. It may also be helpful if you have to mail documents, as many telephone directories also contain mail-stop numbers.

Auditors' Comments

Before starting a project, it is a good idea to know who criticized what. In this instance, auditor comments and management responses can be extremely helpful in determining project strategy. Instead of asking for only last year's comments, ask for the last five years'. In many instances, this information can provide a more in-depth appreciation for both the auditor's and management's position. The more background information you have, the better equipped you will be to deliver a high-quality product.

Prototype Programs

The prototype approach should be considered as a way to reduce the cost of completing a program.

The prototype program should include a recommended corporate contingency policy and strategy, prevention program, incident recovery, and interim processing strategies. The program can be easily expanded or modified, as needed, to fit other locations. There are several benefits to this approach:

- A solid "starter plan" is developed quickly.
- The program can be maintained by in-house personnel.
- Cost is minimal.

AWARENESS AND EDUCATION

Business and Environment

Although all organizations are subject to incited disasters, such as sabotage by a disgruntled employee, some are also subject to disasters peculiar to their business or to their environment. In either event, it is important that senior management be made aware of the specific incidents to which an organization is vulnerable. Consider these examples: ABC Corporation's centralized computer, manufacturing facility, and distribution center are all located in the same building, one-eighth of a mile from the end of a major airport runway; XYZ Company's major production facility is located within five miles of a nuclear power plant; another company has a major distribution facility next to a railroad siding that often contains tank cars of hazardous material. These situations do not take into account numerous businesses in buildings shared with others who do not practice disaster prevention.

Types of Disasters

For the purposes of this book, a disaster is an incident that is

- Caused by a natural event:
  - Flood
  - Hurricane
  - Earthquake
  - Tornado
  - Fire

- Related to environmental problems:
  - Aircraft crash
  - Explosion
  - Localized contamination
  - Hazardous material spill
  - Loss of telephone service
  - Loss of power
  - Strike
  - Water damage
- Incited:
  - Arson
  - Sabotage
  - Vandalism
  - Workplace Violence

Exhibit 5.7 provides a graphic look at the various types of disasters.

Potential Impact on Business

Although it is important to recognize the specific types of disasters that might occur to a given company or business environment, it is equally important to understand what the impact might be under worst-case conditions. The process of uncovering these "exposures" is not unlike a long-range business strategic planning process. Most important is that line managers anticipate problem areas, analyze the exposure, and formulate "what if" interim processing strategies that will ensure business continuity during a stabilization period.

Computers
Given the critical dependence of modern organizations on computerized information, it is clear that a long-term loss of processing capability can be extremely disruptive. Although this would not be fatal for most, some sort of business continuity program should be in place in all organizations. Computers play a key role for many organizations in

EXHIBIT 5.7   Types of Disasters

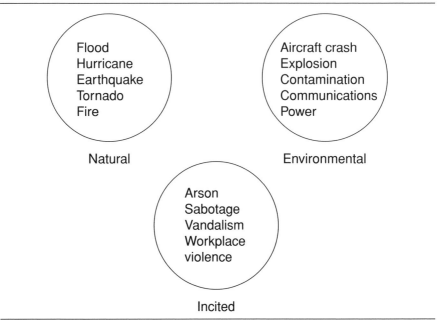

Flood
Hurricane
Earthquake
Tornado
Fire

Natural

Aircraft crash
Explosion
Contamination
Communications
Power

Environmental

Arson
Sabotage
Vandalism
Workplace
violence

Incited

order processing, payroll, work-in-process control, inventory management, billing, and general accounting. Certainly, sound data security and physical security procedures should be in place to help prevent a disaster. In addition, depending on the logistics of a business and the complexity of its computer operations, more comprehensive interim processing strategies may be needed.

Remote Data Communications

Although loss of remote data communications is most likely to happen in conjunction with a disaster that also affects computer operations, it could occur alone. Electronic data interchange (EDI) is increasingly used by customers to enter orders, to check on the status of open orders, and to pay bills. It is also used for order acknowledgment, for transmitting orders to manufacturing facilities, and for invoicing. That is why it is important to have a separate scenario for business continuity in the event that there is a long-term disruption in remote data communications caused by an incident such as putting a backhoe through a communications cable.

Another reason to have a program that will allow a business to continue operating without remote data communications is the assistance it can provide in recovering from a disaster that has also wiped out computer operations. Although it is likely that computer operations can be restored within a two-week period, it may take several more weeks to reconstruct data communication networks. A plan for loss of data communications will allow remote business units to take advantage of the restored computer operations even though communication lines are not yet working.

Voice Communications
Most people are more dependent on voice communications than they realize, and sophisticated computerized telephone systems are becoming more vulnerable daily. Telephones are critical for marketing, customer service, internal communications, and contacting suppliers. Large metropolitan areas increasingly experience periodic failure in telephone systems. In these environments, some type of business continuity program is needed in the event of a loss of telephone service.

Vital Facilities
How would a business continue to function if vital buildings, such as offices, warehouses, distribution centers, and production centers, were not destroyed but could not be accessed for several days? Loss of primary work space is the concern. Fire departments, health agencies, and others can order a building to be quarantined because of structural problems resulting from initial disruptions, hazardous material spills, or contamination. For example, recently a small fire in a facility resulted in chemical contamination. The fire was out in two hours, but the fire department quarantined the facility for four days. If a building is destroyed, insurance is the answer. However, if a building is inaccessible or unusable, alternate business continuity strategies are needed.

Loss of Efficiency
Be careful that individuals developing the program do not *assume* that inefficient solutions are not viable. Quite the contrary! Given the low probability that a disaster will occur, it is important that it be understood

that *loss of efficiency is expected* during a disaster recovery period. Functional managers, supervisors, and other employees will be expected to work longer hours and weekends, and vacations will be deferred until the crisis is over.

Program Objectives

To prevent misunderstanding, provide focus, and facilitate implementation, it is important to define *program objectives.* Contingency planning means different things to different people; therefore, the specific focus and scope of any project needs established parameters before the individuals involved can be expected to buy in to the process. Once agreement on specific objectives is achieved, the development of project strategy and methodology becomes much less subjective. See Exhibit 5.8 for a checklist of program objectives.

Safeguard Assets
Historically, in a business sense, *assets* have meant physical assets, such as buildings, fixtures, vehicles, and equipment. In recent years, three new types of assets have joined the group:

1. Computerized data
2. Computer programs
3. Computer processing capability

Although traditional insurance programs protect physical assets at reasonable premium rates, there is no cost-effective insurance policy that

---

EXHIBIT 5.8 Contingency Program Objectives

- Prevent disasters from occurring.
- Contain the impact of a disaster if one does happen.
- Provide an organized response to a disaster/incident.
- Minimize disruptions to cash flow.
- Provide alternate ways to service customer orders.
- Prevent a significant long-term loss of market share.

covers computerized data, computer programs, or computer processing capability. The reason for the lack of traditional insurance coverage
in these three areas lies in the lack of credible probability statistics on
which to calculate risk.

The solution to protecting computerized data and computer programs against loss is to periodically make backup copies and physically store them away from the normal operating environment.
Following a disaster, such as a fire, it would then be possible to restore
computerized data and reconstruct beginning balances.

Computer hardware presents a different problem. Unlike software,
most replacement computer equipment can be acquired from manufacturers, leasing companies, or brokers. The question is, under emergency
conditions, how long would it take to restore temporary computer processing capability? Most management information systems (MIS)
directors are confident that, given unlimited resources to get the job
done, they could expect to have computer operations restored within 10
calendar days. It is also conceivable that a temporary configuration
might have to be leased until a permanent system is delivered. However, the resources saved by avoiding a computer hot-site agreement for
40 years will more than offset the cost of a two-step restoration. A business continuity program should ensure that there will not be a significant deterioration in either cash flow or customer service during a
stabilization period.

Prevention
Preventive measures and detection devices are the most cost-effective
deterrents to disaster. They reduce the probability that a disaster will
occur and help to minimize the impact if one does occur. Preventive
steps, such as an annual review and correction program for potential
fire hazards, installation and monitoring of physical access control
procedures, and installation of backup power sources, are integral to
any worthwhile program. Devices such as fire detection and alarm systems, temperature-control alarm systems, and suppression systems
(such as sprinklers) are most effective. Their presence, in combination
with other sound contingency planning practices, will help to reduce
insurance premiums. A prevention program should indicate specific
responsibility for prevention and detection procedures.

Organized Response

Immediately following a disaster is the incident recovery period, during which are numerous issues that deserve immediate attention. What specifically is to be done will depend on damage assessment and the prognosis for recovery. There is no need to attempt to spell out precisely what will be done in various combinations of events. Rather, it is important to have a list of tasks, such as *media control,* and specific individuals assigned to be responsible for those activities. It is also important that there be some sort of ongoing audit to ensure compliance.

Business Continuity

As stated previously, the objective of interim processing strategies is to keep the business running, not the technology. In this regard, it is important to remember that for many years products were produced and shipped without the aid of computer systems. Systematizing ensured the consistent application of previously established procedures, facilitated the efficient processing of large volumes of data, and stored data so they could be manipulated, sorted, collated, and summarized for different purposes. *Efficiency* is the operative word. However, there is no reason that most organizations could not return to *selective* manual processing or use personal computers to keep track of vital transactions during a stabilization period.

Loss of efficiency during a stabilization period can be addressed in several ways. Among the solutions are: processing documents selectively and holding specific types until operations are restored, temporarily relaxing processing requirements, adding temporary help to perform increased workloads, and working overtime and deferring vacations until temporary processing capability can be restored. Exhibit 5.9 lists the four ways to compensate for loss of efficiency.

EXHIBIT 5.9   Ways to Compensate for Loss of Efficiency

- Selectively process transactions.
- Relax standard operating procedures.
- Add temporary personnel to deal with expected inefficiency.
- Schedule overtime; defer vacations and business travel.

Cash Flow, Customer Service, and Market Share

One of the best ways to determine which business activities are essential, and which are not, is to anticipate their potential impact in three key result areas: getting the cash in the bank, shipping product, and maintaining customer base. Still, because almost every business activity can claim to have *some* impact in one or more of these areas, a qualifying modifier is needed. It is therefore appropriate to define as essential business functions those activities that can have a significant impact on cash flow, servicing customer orders, or maintaining market share.

CASH FLOW

One of the most important objectives of a sound contingency program is to address the importance of cash flow. But is it essential to maintain the same rate of cash flow as before the disaster? Perhaps not, but it *is* important to *prevent a significant deterioration in cash flow* during a disaster recovery period. There may be several causes for a negative impact on cash flow:

- Manual billing errors may result in a loss of revenue.
- Selective billings may be intentionally deferred until computer processing capability is restored.
- Collection activity may be deferred because accurate account status is temporarily not available.

The potential revenue lost to these causes is small compared with the cost of continuing to provide redundant processing capability over a number of years. Some deterioration in cash flow should be expected and accepted as a legitimate cost of a more cost-effective contingency program strategy.

The most important objective during a stabilization period is to get cash into the bank immediately, deferring cash application until after computer operations are restored. This can have an adverse impact on credit approval, but because it is cost-justified to defer cash collection for a short period of time, many organizations elect to use alternate procedures to approve credit during a disaster recovery period. One of the accepted alternate practices is to prepare a short list of problem accounts and manually research payment and booking activity in approving credit for new orders. Another is for a business to intentionally relax credit approval for a few days, knowing that in some instances collection could be a problem.

CUSTOMER SERVICE

Another area that deserves attention is that of servicing customer orders. During the stabilization period, customer service will be less efficient and the status of work-in-process may not be completely accurate. What does this mean? It means that instead of answering inquiries instantly by calling up a screen reflecting job status, other methods will have to be used. It may mean working overtime, and it will probably mean delays in responding to inquiries. You may have to hedge some commitments, but most customers will be understanding if you explain your predicament to them.

MARKET SHARE

A third issue is the prevention of a *significant* long-term loss in market share. If a permanent drop in market share is a real risk, then the cost of providing redundant technology may be justified. If a long-term loss of market share would not be the result, then consideration should be given to enduring a short-term drop in market share in view of the long-term savings achieved by eliminating monthly technology backup subscription fees. Exhibit 5.10 highlights contingency planning key result areas.

Insurance Considerations

An essential component of a risk management program is insurance. The role of insurance in protecting against loss of physical assets, such

---

EXHIBIT 5.10   Key Result Areas

- Prevent significant long-term deterioration in market share.
- Deposit cash.
- Defer cash application until normal processing capability is restored.
- Anticipate a severe drop in efficiency.

as buildings and equipment, is clear. However, using insurance policies to protect against the loss of cash flow, the ability to service customers, or the ability to maintain market share is often not practical. In addition to high premium rates, the primary concern is the inability to prove that losses of this type were *solely* the result of a specific disaster and not caused by management practices or marketplace conditions. So, for the most part, organizations have rejected insurance policies as a solution to these three issues. However, the extent to which your organization is dealing with disaster prevention and disaster recovery issues *will* affect business interruption premium rates. A discussion of the key elements that affect that rate structure follows.

Premium Consequences

The primary function of business insurance is to provide a hedge against loss or damage. A contingency program, however, has three objectives:

1. Prevent disasters from happening
2. Provide an organized response to a disaster situation
3. Ensure business continuity during a stabilization period

Insurance is intended to provide funds for replacement of *tangible* assets, whereas a contingency program describes how a business will survive. The presence of a sound contingency program will have a direct bearing on insurance premiums (see Exhibit 5.11).

EXHIBIT 5.11   Insurance Premium Rate Considerations

- Management commitment
- On-site controls
- Building construction
- Environment
- Business operation
- Inspection
- Sprinklers
- Water supply

What Impacts Insurance Premiums

Many ask the question: "Will insurance premiums be less with a contingency program?" The answer is yes. The next question is: "How much will insurance premiums drop if we develop a contingency program?" The answer is 5 to 10 percent. The last question is: "Specifically, what do insurance providers look for in evaluating a contingency program?" They look at eight areas:

1. *Management commitment.* Evidence of management support can be demonstrated by policy and strategy statements endorsed by senior management, periodic memos or letters from senior executives concerning the need to be attentive to disaster prevention, and the presence of an ongoing employee awareness and education program.

2. *On-site controls and procedures.* Good housekeeping and preventive maintenance programs fit into this category. Insurance agents will observe such things as the presence or absence of No Smoking signs, evidence of ongoing inspection and maintenance procedures, and the extent to which storage areas are free of litter.

3. *Building construction and use-code compliance.* The objective of assessing building construction and use-code compliance is to evaluate the extent to which facilities are in compliance with building codes and the appropriateness of the business to the physical structure it occupies. For instance, insurance companies are likely to charge a higher premium if chemicals are produced in a building originally designed for shoe manufacturing.

4. *External exposure.* The accumulation of dried brush behind a building would be a negative. Similarly, the nearby presence of a fireworks plant or a facility's close proximity to a railroad siding where carloads of cleaning chemicals are stored periodically would not be good.

5. *Special hazards.* Operations such as spray painting and the use of toxic chemicals and highly volatile solutions will count as a negative. If these are present, prevention and detection devices that help prevent an incident, or at least minimize the impact of one, should be installed.

6. *Supervisory inspection procedures.* A program of periodic inspections by supervisors to verify that procedures for prevention and detection are being enforced counts as a plus.

7. *Sprinkler systems.* The presence of sprinkler systems and periodic testing of those systems in office buildings, plants, and warehouses is important to insurance companies.

8. *Water supply.* Insurance companies like to know that there is a fire hydrant accessible to a facility and that there is a sufficient supply of water and enough pressure to fight a fire for a reasonable period of time.

Although it may be difficult for an insurance agent to attribute a specific value to each of these considerations, it is certain that in aggregate they will impact insurance premium rates.

How Much Detail?

How much detail should a contingency program have? Three issues will help to determine the amount of detail covered in a program:

1. Number of different levels of disaster included in the planning process
2. Adequacy of the education and awareness program
3. Documentation format

There are basically two choices when it comes to the number of levels of disaster planning to be included.

1. Address multiple levels, such as a one- to three-day outage, a three- to seven-day outage, and a one- to two-week outage, or
2. Develop strategies for a worst-case scenario, with the understanding that parts of it could be used for lesser disasters. With this approach, you will have only one strategy to develop, test, and maintain, without significantly degrading quality.

There is a tendency to look at program development as a procedure-writing project and to include detail normally contained in standard operating procedures. However, the objective of interim processing strategies is *not* to write procedures, but to document and communicate guidelines that can be used to ensure cash flow and support customer service until normal operations are restored. Detailed instructions are not needed. If and when a disaster does occur, people are certainly not going to take time to read and follow detailed instructions. Individuals responsible for making decisions following a disaster need only a check-list of tasks that should not be overlooked. It is virtually impossible and a waste of time to attempt to anticipate every combination of disasters that might occur and to specify exactly what steps should be taken in each instance. The important point is to monitor program development closely to make certain that excessive detail is avoided.

In programs developed by outside specialists, the main cause of excessive detail is the fee basis of their contract. When consultants work on a per-diem basis, there is a tendency to:

- Spend more time in meetings
- Write voluminous, detailed reports

Per-diem consulting contracts are counterproductive in developing contingency programs. To reduce a consultant's inclination to provide unnecessarily detailed programs, make certain that the fee is fixed and that satisfaction will be determined by the quality of the solutions rather than by the amount of detail. Then monitor the data-gathering process to make certain this philosophy is communicated to the individuals doing the work.

In developing a contingency program, a common mistake is to waste valuable time attempting to document solutions to hypothetical situations that might not occur. Although it is tempting to try to find answers to various combinations of scenarios, this contributes little to the value of the program, increases development costs, and creates a maintenance nightmare.

Establishing a Firm Foundation

The single greatest deterrent to developing cost-effective contingency programs is the lack of an effective awareness and education program.

Senior management must be made aware of these facts:

- The business is exposed to sudden disaster.

- It makes good business sense to have interim processing strategies as a point of reference should a disaster actually happen.

- The contingency planning strategy is to protect market share, cash flow, and the ability to service customers during a stabilization period.

- The methodology to be used in program development should specifically be designed to yield cost-effective solution.

Department managers need to be informed of these facts:

- Senior management considers development of interim processing strategies the responsibility of line managers.

- Participation in program development will not be disruptive to their normal operations.

- Department managers have a responsibility to stockholders and senior management to make certain that, because of the low probability of a disaster's occurring, their plans reflect bare-bones needs.

Key Result Areas

A well-thought-out contingency program should: have the approval of key players, be flexible, contain a maintenance process, be cost effective, emphasize business continuity, provide for an organized response, assign specific responsibilities, and include a test program.

See Exhibit 5.12 for a checklist of desirable program characteristics.

EXHIBIT 5.12   Characteristics of a Good Program

- Workable—developed by first-line supervisors
- Cost-effective—in relation to low probability
- Flexible—same program can be used for any disaster
- Easy to maintain—keep it simple
- Deals in strategies—not detailed procedures

Approval
The program must be acceptable to internal auditors, outside auditors, senior management, customers, and suppliers.

Flexibility
The program should consist of strategies rather than details tied to specific disaster situations, so that line managers have the latitude to exercise judgment when the time comes to implement any portion of the program.

Maintenance
Avoid unnecessary detail so that the program can easily be updated.

Cost-Effectiveness
Project planning should emphasize the need to minimize program development costs, redundant backup processing subscription fees, and maintenance and testing costs.

Business Continuity
The program must ensure business continuity during a stabilization period.

Organized Response
The program should provide a checklist of issues that need attention immediately following a disaster. It should include lists of phone numbers and addresses of individuals to be contacted.

Responsibility
Specific individuals should be assigned responsibility for each issue that requires attention during a stabilization period.

Testing
Testing with user preparedness reviews and backup procedures verification should be performed at specific time intervals. The program should state frequencies of testing and document the testing methodology.

Convincing Others

Selling is success! If one is to be successful in obtaining the commitment of senior management, the resources needed to do the job, and the cooperation of department managers, the value of contingency planning must be emphasized. Once the persons involved accept the project values, they in turn become sponsors and advocates.

The list of those who need to be sold is impressive: senior management, audit committee members, internal auditors, outside auditors, division managers, department heads, first-line supervisors, and vendors. The problem is that many involved in contingency planning have had little sales training, and yet this is one of the most critical elements of success. If you are able to master *the process of successful selling,* you will succeed where others have failed. Successful selling consists of addressing two areas:

1. Organizational needs
2. Personal needs

Organizational Needs

The first step in using organizational needs to sell contingency planning is to select a specific individual who needs to be sold—the president, an auditor, or another person.

The second step is to classify the sales target as someone who is primarily oriented to *cost, image,* or *business requirement.*

The cost-oriented individual is primarily concerned with cost-related issues. No matter what the subject, this person is interested in items such as cost justification, return on investment, or other cost-related issues. Image-oriented individuals are most concerned with what others think, such as auditors, customers, senior management, and suppliers. A "business requirement" person is primarily concerned with getting the job done.

Although many individuals may evidence more than one of these characteristics, one of them will normally be dominant and easy to spot in most business-related discussions. For instance, ask a department manager to explain his or her long-range department plans. As the manager describes *what* is planned, ask "Why?" Listen carefully:

The manager will reveal a specific orientation to one of the three categories: cost, image, or business requirement.

The third step is to select a benefit that will result when the program is completed, one that is related to cost, image, or business requirement (depending on the type of individual you are trying to sell). In other words, when addressing a cost-oriented person, select a cost-related benefit.

The fourth step is to ask the sales target to describe the perceived value in the benefit you have selected. It does no good to have sales targets nod their heads yes. The person must explain the perceived value in his or her own words. Therefore, the question must be posed in a structured format, such as: "Can you tell me in your own words why you feel it is important that our contingency program be cost-effective?" The sales target has then been put in a position where he or she cannot do anything but support the project. Furthermore, through the process of stating what is perceived to be valuable, the sales targets in turn sell themselves.

The fifth step is to "close the sale" by describing how the project strategy and program development methodology will achieve the specific benefit you chose to discuss. The same process is repeated with each sales target, with care taken to select a benefit that matches that person's orientation: cost, image, or business requirement.

See Exhibit 5.13 for a summary of the organizational needs selling technique.

Personal Needs

Understanding the ego of your sales target can be extremely useful in selling the chosen approach to contingency planning. By understanding

---

EXHIBIT 5.13   Steps in Organizational Needs Selling

1. Select a sales target.
2. Classify sales target as either cost, image, or business requirement oriented.
3. Select appropriate benefit to discuss.
4. Have sales targets describe in their own words the value they perceive in the benefit you have mentioned.
5. Explain how your methodology will help achieve that benefit.

your sales target's personal needs, you can appeal to those needs in your sales pitch and achieve outstanding success simply because you paid attention to those needs. The next discussion defines six ego classifications and describes how you can use this insight to improve your selling skills.

1. *Team player.* Likes and values cooperation, is concerned with what others think, likes to serve on committees, and wants consensus.

2. *Recognition.* Values praise, likes to have high visibility, and has certificates or awards posted on the walls of his or her office.

3. *Structure.* Believes in a defined process, is concerned with details, and feels planning is the key to success.

4. *Results.* Thinks that the end justifies the means, dislikes detail, and is goal oriented.

5. *Control.* Likes power, wants to dominate, and feels that no matter who calls a meeting or what the subject is, he or she has a God-given right to do most of the talking.

6. *Low risk.* Attracted to cost-benefit analysis, resistant to change, and likes guarantees.

Selling Process

The first step is to classify the sales target as being dominant in one of the preceding categories. The last step is to make the person feel confident that the program development methodology will accommodate his or her needs. For instance, when talking to a *team player,* you might say something like: "Susan, I want you to know that I understand the importance of making sure other managers are supportive of our program, and as we develop solutions, we will review them with others to gain their concurrence."

This process works only on a one-to-one basis. The objective is to make the sales target feel comfortable that his or her personal needs will be addressed as a part of the program development methodology. This is called selling, and it can be extremely effective in obtaining support, in securing the resources to get the job done, and in marshaling support for involvement in program development.

Executive Briefings

Concise executive briefings are an excellent way to sell senior management and department managers on overall corporate policy and expectations, implementation strategy, and program development methodology. However, in structuring these presentations, remember two things: While contingency planning is important to you, executive briefing attendees will have a limited attention span as soon as you mention *contingency planning*; therefore, use bullets and key words in your presentation and refrain from lengthy explanations (or else you will put your audience to sleep); also, tailor your presentation to senior management to focus on corporate policy and implementation strategy, and tailor the presentation to department managers to emphasize program development methodology. Key components of an executive briefing are:

- Corporate contingency planning policy and strategy
- Disaster recovery life cycle
- Prevention
- Incident recovery
- Interim processing strategies
- Corporate concerns
- Departmental issues

Corporate Contingency Program Policy and Strategy
The briefing should focus on developing separate programs for each facility, including restoring communications technology as well as restoring computer processing capability. It should clarify that interim processing strategies will be developed under existing conditions and will not assume any "planned" safeguards that do not exist at program development time. Programs can be modified in future years to reflect any environmental changes that have occurred; they should not anticipate planned changes!

Contingency Program Phases
Contingency programs should address only three time periods; prevention programs, that is, the time before a disaster occurs; incident recovery,

that is, the first 24 or 48 hours immediately following an incident; and interim processing, that is, the period when the building is assumed, for contingency planning purposes, to be inaccessible and/or the period during which normal computer processing capability may not be operable. Where, when, and how normal operations will be restored should not be included because those issues cannot be addressed until the specific and unique nature of a given disaster has been evaluated. The objective is to permit operations to be stabilized while senior management decides when, how, and where normal operations will be resumed.

Prevention

Although department managers will not be involved in developing a prevention program, they should understand the part it plays in the completed program. This part of the briefing should take only a few minutes, but sharing it with the department managers will make them feel involved and encourage them to contribute when it comes time to develop interim processing strategies. It should be explained that a prevention program is a combination of procedures and practices, such as physical security measures that limit access to a building and specific areas, which tend to reduce the likelihood of a disaster. It also includes systematic measures, such as storing computerized information off-site so it can be recovered and used after a disaster, which in turn limits the impact of a disaster.

Incident Recovery

It should be explained that incident recovery covers a time period of approximately 24 to 48 hours immediately following an incident. It ensures an organized response to a facility-related disaster and provides for the rapid restoration of communications and computer processing capability. It addresses issues such as damage assessment, crisis management, relocation strategy, notification, media management, and physical and data security concerns immediately after a disaster has occurred.

Interim Processing

It is in this area that the cooperation and participation of department managers is critical to success. If they feel threatened that their opinions do not really matter, or sense that their involvement is perceived as superficial, their resistance will harden; their answers will be evasive; and they will not open up to help in identifying options to survive during a stabilization period. Remember, although department heads are not willing to give up the benefits of computer systems under normal operating conditions, they can almost always find alternate methods to keep the place running for a week or two without those systems, if necessary. So ask, probe, and listen.

Corporate Concerns

Senior management's objectives in the event of a physical disaster are to do whatever is necessary to service customers, retain market share, and maintain cash flow until normal operations can be resumed. Senior management understands that immediately following a disaster, inefficiencies will negatively impact customer service levels and there may also be some temporary loss of market share and cash flow.

Departmental Issues

Department managers have sole responsibility for determining what strategies should be used to maintain continuity of operations following a disaster. But senior management is also concerned that department managers' time will be taken away from their regular responsibilities to develop these interim processing strategies. Be sure to point out that, to the contrary, a "surgical process" will be used to minimize the amount of time department managers will spend on the project, and that all notes and write-ups will be done by the contingency planner, not the manager. Department managers should review and approve the strategies.

BUSINESS IMPACT ANALYSIS

Objective

In conducting a business impact analysis (BIA), it is important to let others know the context in which the questions are asked. It makes a big difference in the answers and will have a subtle but profound impact on the cost of developing and maintaining interim processing strategies. Individuals who usually insist that they could not do without a report for more than three days under normal conditions might be willing to do without it for three weeks during a stabilization period. Unless time is taken before the questioning process begins to ensure that the mind-set is *survival* rather than *business as usual,* the motivation to pursue cost-effective solutions will be missing. An awareness and education program is the vital first step to set the stage so that when questions about impact on business are asked, the responses are more helpful in arriving at cost-effective solutions.

The purpose of a BIA is not to document potential loss so that management will make contingency planning a high priority, nor is its purpose to cost-justify redundant processing capability. (See Exhibit 5.14.)

It is not realistic to indicate that a disaster "will result in a loss of $82,000 a day" while assuming that nothing would be done to continue operations. If there is a disaster that temporarily destroys normal processing capability, management staff will automatically search for ways to keep shipping product. They may not be efficient, but they will give it a go. To assume that managers would sit on their hands while their business deteriorates before their eyes is absurd; however, that is exactly the position that many consultants take when conducting a BIA. They are trying so hard to sell backup processing that they misrepresent management's resourcefulness to respond and survive under adverse conditions. This can be particularly true of consulting groups owned by organizations in the backup technology business, as well as vendors who offer backup technology and also claim to provide "independent" consulting assistance in business resumption planning. Instead of encouraging clients to develop more cost-effective solutions, many of them sell hot-site agreements.

EXHIBIT 5.14   Objectives of a Business Impact Analysis

- Position functional managers so that they are comfortable participating in the program development process.
- Educate functional managers so that they understand the economics and importance of searching for cost-effective solutions.
- Encourage the evaluation of all options before considering redundant processing.

Another potential problem with conducting a BIA is that we get the wrong answer because we ask the wrong question. Although we must find out what business functions are most critical, we should not ask, "What is most critical?" Nor should we ask, "What do you need to keep going?" or "How long could you operate without?" Instead, it is important to go through a process that will make department managers aware of the extremely high cost of providing processing redundancy on a continuing basis, understand the low probability of a disaster's happening, understand the relatively short period of time before operations would be restored, and realize the need for their participation in program development. Then work with them to develop "what if" interim processing strategies by asking the right question: *How could you survive in the face of such loss?*

What Is Really Critical?

The intent behind the question "What is critical?" is to discover which technology should be given restoration priority following a disaster. The problem is that finding out what is critical can be accomplished only as a result of the investigatory process.

To arrive at a conclusion, these four questions must be answered:

1. What are the business functions performed?
2. Which business functions are vital (e.g., can have a *significant* impact on cash flow or servicing customer orders)?
3. What alternative methods could be used to continue those functions during a stabilization period (regardless of how inefficient they might be)?
4. After eliminating those vital business functions for which there are alternate methods of support, what business functions are left?

The residual of this process is what is really critical.

A Word of Caution

It is virtually impossible to cost-justify an amount to be spent on developing a contingency program. This is because only a small fraction of disasters have a significant impact on business continuity, and there have not been enough of them to establish credible probability statistics for cost-justification. The important thing to remember is that a disaster can happen.

Awareness and Education

What are the mechanics of awareness and education? This is a two-step process of changing a mind-set from business as usual to survival and emphasizing the need for cost-effective solutions, given the low probability that a disaster will occur. Exhibit 5.15 compares disaster recovery period philosophies.

Mind-Set

Before exploring the alternate methods that might be used to support vital business functions during a stabilization period, it is important to understand that the objective is to do the minimum to stay in business and, at the same time, prevent a significant long-term drop in market share. The key to cost-effective solutions is to make certain that this philosophy is in place before the rest of the process is set in motion. Exhibit 5.16 lists guidelines for establishing the proper mind-set.

EXHIBIT 5.15   Comparison of Stabilization Period Philosophies

Business as Usual	
Advantages:	• Work 8 to 5 • Vacations permitted • Follow normal procedures
Disadvantages:	• Costs millions of dollars over years • Testing disruptive
Survival	
Advantages:	• Large cost prevention/saving • Business continuity is user responsibility
Disadvantages:	• Drop in efficiency • Use alternate procedures • Overtime will be required

---

EXHIBIT 5.16   Establishing the Proper Mind-Set

- Discuss business continuity objectives.
- Focus on essential business functions.
- Look for unique requirements for individual business units.
- Assure functional managers that admitting they could survive a stabilization period without normal technology will not be interpreted as meaning they could do without it on a continuing basis.

Education

It is equally important to realize that if it becomes necessary to implement these interim processing strategies, it will be for only a short period of time, probably a few days or weeks. This knowledge provides a comfort level to those faced with answering the question: How would we survive? They are much more likely to suggest alternate methods if they understand that the window is small. It is also important for them to understand that the probability is remote and that the high cost of redundancy demands low-cost, bare-bones solutions. Exhibit 5.17 provides information on why education is important in developing a contingency program.

Cost

There are four areas in which costs can easily get out of control:

1. Program development
2. Computer hot-site subscription fees

EXHIBIT 5.17   Components of an Education Program

- There is a low probability of a major localized disaster.
- The cumulative cost of redundant processing capability is high.
- Cost-effective solutions are the key.
- Functional managers have primary responsibility for developing interim processing strategies.
- Data processing and other utility providers concentrate on restoring service.
- Survival is the objective, not business as usual.

---

3. Program maintenance

4. Computer testing

Without a professionally directed awareness and education program as the first module of program development, the cost containment battle may be lost. Development of "what if" interim processing strategies is a sensitive issue that can move dramatically in one of two directions, depending on the mind-set of functional managers. Without a sound education program, interim processing strategies will be inordinately costly because department managers will convince themselves of the indispensability of high-tech equipment. They will insist on its immediate recovery because they will not have been educated on the need to search for more cost-effective solutions and because they assume that efficiency during a stabilization period is cost-justified. A strong educational program for functional managers is needed so that they do not assume high-tech equipment is the only viable short-term solution and that they recognize that loss of efficiency is to be expected during a stabilization period. If they are not so educated, the danger of committing to exorbitant monthly subscription fees for redundant high-tech backup processing capability is high. Furthermore, testing will be difficult if not impossible, and it will be a constant source of criticism by auditors and an irritant to business unit managers. Simple, cost-effective interim processing strategies need only simple testing procedures. Keep the solutions simple and straightforward.

Regulatory Agency Reporting Requirements

An example of the importance of mind-set in program development is the manner in which information is gathered concerning issues such as normal reporting requirements. The mind-set in which this information is developed can play a large part in determining whether a program is cost effective. For example, you may ask the individual responsible for report preparation what the deadline is for submitting report A to the federal government. The individual replies that government regulations require the report to be submitted no later than the fifth working day of the month and adds a personal comment: "We must meet this reporting requirement."

In this context, it is easy to assume that this report due date will continue to be valid during a stabilization period. However, this is probably not the case. A good example is that after a major bank fire, the controller of the currency waived such reporting requirements. Never *assume* that regular reporting requirements will have to be sustained during a stabilization period.

Window

A window, for our purposes, is the time period during which an outage is likely to exist. Lack of historical information makes this a real issue when it comes to losing computer processing capability. Most computer directors are reasonably assured that under conditions of emergency or disaster, a window of one to two weeks is reasonable, provided management has authorized monies to restore operations quickly. Vendors would be pulled out of meetings, overtime would be authorized, replacement equipment would be air-freighted immediately, and installation specialists would remain on-site 24 hours a day until service was restored. Vacations for critical technical personnel would be canceled, and they would also be available 24 hours a day. Replacement computers would be temporarily installed in any available area, such as the cafeteria, warehouse, or some other space. Air-conditioning units would be placed in windows as needed, computer operators might have to step over cables for a few months, and working conditions would be less than ideal. However, product would get out the door and cash flow could be maintained.

As far as remote data communications are concerned, consider some alternatives. Although we have become accustomed to the luxury of remote data communications, most business functions could survive by using alternate and less efficient communications procedures for a few days or weeks until normal data communication links are restored. Overnight courier services are reliable and available to most locations. They could be used to send inquiries or data to a restored computer operation that temporarily operates in a batch mode. The entries or inquiries could be data entered using hard-wired terminals at the restored site and responses express-mailed or phoned to remote facilities. Although this might cause a 24-hour delay in answering inquiries, it would have no serious impact on maintaining market share.

SELECTING A METHODOLOGY

Philosophy

The Program Process is a combination of an innovative consulting philosophy and a unique contingency planning methodology.

My opinion is that per-diem consulting is counterproductive and not in a client's best interest. This is because it: (1) encourages spending more time than necessary on an assignment; (2) disrupts operations with many drawn-out group meetings; (3) results in thick and unnecessarily detailed reports; and (4) ends with a staggering consulting bill. Because per-diem consulting fees are unexpectedly high for "first-phase" assignments, many times clients, in frustration or annoyance, terminate a consultant's work and never reap any benefits.

Cost-effective contingency planning work is done on a fixed-fee basis, which: (1) limits the time spent on an assignment; (2) minimizes disruption to operations with brief one-on-one meetings; (3) includes concise reports; and (4) ends with a consulting fee that was fixed at the outset.

This contingency planning methodology evolved from a market research study of traditional disaster recovery planning practices that disclosed five problems and weaknesses:

1. Using a flawed business impact analysis to focus on what would not get done following a computer disaster, without adequately exploring alternates for maintaining business continuity until computer processing is restored

2. Addressing unnecessary issues

3. Documenting endlessly detailed procedures

4. Failing to develop interim processing strategies to service customers if a facility is temporarily inaccessible

5. Failing to establish reasonable outage windows prior to developing interim processing strategies with department heads.

It is standard practice to:

1. Recommend a corporate contingency planning policy and strategy designed to minimize program development costs.
2. Establish reasonable outage windows for computer and building disasters.
3. Develop interim processing strategies with department heads for operating until computer processing is restored and/or until a facility is accessible.
4. Develop interim processing strategies that identify *what* will be done but allows managers flexibility in deciding *how* things will be done, depending on the specific nature of a given disaster.
5. Exclude issues that can reasonably be expected to be resolved at the time of a disaster, without preplanning.

Why It Has Worked
This process has worked because it is simple, straightforward, and comprehensive, and, at least partially, because of experience in systems and procedures; finance and accounting; manufacturing and materials control; and consulting protocol with a major international consulting firm. This experience has enabled development of a well-thought-out corporate contingency program policy and strategy; establishment of reasonable outage windows as a framework for evaluating alternate interim processing strategies; negotiation of practical interim processing strategies with department managers; and completion of a prototype program in 30 days.

Creating the right perspective is a crucial first phase in business continuity planning, the stage at which entirely too many otherwise sound plans have foundered. It involves the sensitive encounter of first-line supervisors in user departments. Discomfort, insecurity, even fear, are mixed with their logical and professional responses. If these factors are not understood and carefully dealt with, they can quickly harden into resistance or evasion.

This process is to deal with these issues in ways that respect both the individuals involved and the delicate structure of an organization's policy. In dealing with first-line managers, it is important to listen very carefully to their information and ideas. They quickly perceive that their opinions count and will play a serious role in evolving a program.

Once you have gained acceptance and understand the workings of any unique business functions, you can then anticipate specific problems that could accompany a disaster.

In the area of data processing, everything is precise: restore/restart procedures, record lengths, data security, and backup instructions. If contingency planning is presented as a data processing problem, solutions tend to become exceedingly precise and painfully detailed. If contingency planning is presented as an interim processing issue, solutions tend to be less complex.

Once department managers understand that they are responsible for developing "what if" interim processing strategies, they demand answers to some key questions. An important part of problem definition is a prognosis of recovery. Is processing likely to be inoperative for a few hours or for several months? The situation may be likened to one in which someone explains that you are going on a trip and then asks whether you would like to walk, bike, drive, take a bus or a train, or fly. Before answering the question, you need to know *where* you are going. Similarly, users of computer systems are entitled to know, in the event that the entire system needs to be replaced, the estimated time it will take to restore operations.

Setting the Stage for Success

There is a saying among golfers that "most bets are won on the first tee," meaning that negotiating a fair chance to collect after the eighteenth hole can be the key to winning. Similarly, properly defining corporate contingency program philosophy, objectives, cost constraints, assumptions, and expectations is essential to timely completion of a program. While subsequent years' updating can be done by most staff, the initial program needs to be orchestrated by a specialist experienced in this process.

Cost-effective contingency planning does not entail conducting a costly business impact analysis for the purpose of gaining consensus on what computer systems are more critical than others under normal operating conditions. It is a meaningless and costly exercise whose purpose many times is to compensate outside consultants while they become oriented to your operations or enable in-house systems staff who normally deal exclusively with computer programs to become knowledgeable of operating methods, procedures, and logistics. A business impact analysis is a carryover from anachronistic large mainframe environments where all systems were contained on one computer and could be restored individually. Today, critical core systems run on a separate computer and are interdependent and cannot be restored individually. If all the critical core systems are restored at once, why is there a need for a costly business impact study? Certainly not to preestablish what data will be entered first or second, because that is an issue that can easily be directed by the information systems department.

What is critical under normal operating conditions has little to do with being able to maintain business continuity during a stabilization period when the computer is not functioning for a few days. A more productive approach is to present a disaster scenario in which computer processing is assumed to be inoperable for 10 working days, and then let department managers explain how various business functions could be accomplished successfully, if not efficiently, under those conditions. If under those conditions customers can still be served and market share maintained, then there is no critical issue to resolve.

Cost-effective contingency planing does not include developing a computer recovery strategy as the first step. It is counterproductive, based on erroneous assumptions, and can result in proposing to pay costly computer hot-site subscription fees when they are not needed. A computer recovery strategy should be considered only after all functional departments have documented options for surviving while computer processing capability is inoperable. Only then is it possible to know what heroic measures should be taken to restore computer operations in one day versus three days, three days versus five days, and so on. The mistake of developing the computer recovery strategy first is usually caused by focusing on keeping the computer running instead of keeping the *business* running. It is also caused by assuming that while the computer is essential under normal operating conditions, it must be essential for 10 days following a computer disaster. Because many organizations commit the error of developing a computer recovery strategy before business continuity strategies are documented, many companies are paying monthly computer hot-site fees and incurring annual computer hot-site testing programs that are overkill.

Program Requirements

Four objectives of a program are:

1. Institutionalize whatever steps should be taken to prevent the likelihood of a disaster, including minimizing the impact if one does occur.
2. Document how the organization will continue despite a disaster.
3. Assign responsibilities to specific individuals.
4. Provide for review to ensure compliance.

See Exhibit 5.18 for a list of these requirements.

Prevention

Records retention and computer backup procedures should be designed to ensure that beginning balances and status indicators provide a reasonably accurate starting point for interim processing strategies used during a stabilization period. Procedures for data security and physical security should be designed to lessen exposure to the likelihood of a disaster and to minimize the impact of a disaster if one does occur.

EXHIBIT 5.18   Program Requirements

- Prevention—physical security, data security, and the like
- Recovery—of essential business functions
- Accountability—during normal operations, emergency response, and stabilization period
- Compliance audits—institutionalize business continuity programs

Recovery

Well-thought-out strategies must be developed to facilitate timely and orderly recovery from disaster conditions. Most important is that business is able to continue. Next, whatever processing capability or facility is damaged or destroyed must be replaced with dispatch.

Accountability

Specific individuals should be responsible for certain tasks during the following periods:

- Prevention (the period of time before a disaster occurs)
- Incident recovery (the hours immediately following a disaster/incident when specific survival scenarios must be implemented quickly, often without complete information)
- Interim processing period (the period of time during which alternate business continuity strategies are in effect)

Audit

To maintain integrity, contingency programs must be audited and tested periodically. Backup procedures should be checked to ensure that proper information is retained and backed up at reasonable intervals. Information should be stored in an off-site location, physically separate from the facility being protected and in a format that can be processed without modification. Interim processing strategies for processing orders and shipping the product must undergo periodic preparedness reviews to examine the likelihood of their working when the time comes for implementation.

Program Development Steps

The goal is to produce a realistic interim processing program based on practical interim processing strategies. Evolving these strategies requires a careful, comprehensive process, which involves four distinct steps:

1. *Positioning* program development participants so that they are in the right mind-set to contribute to the development of interim processing strategies that are most cost-effective

2. *Educating* participants on the low probability of a disaster's happening and helping them to understand the low probability, as well as the high cost of providing 100 percent redundant processing capability, which means that they must look hard for low-cost solutions and be willing to live with temporary inconveniences and inefficiencies

3. *Developing interim processing strategies* that show how each business function would operate during a stabilization period

4. *Documenting* strategies in a concise format that is easy to read, easy to understand, and easy to maintain

See Exhibit 5.19 for a checklist of program development steps.

Key Tasks

Focus on Essential Business Functions, Not Technology

Essential business functions are defined as those that have a *significant* impact on either cash flow or servicing customer orders. Business functions that do not fit this model should not be considered essential, regardless of how much users insist they are critical. It is often necessary to have lengthy discussions before agreement is reached to persuade users that a particular function is not essential to maintaining cash flow or servicing customer orders. An activity that makes order processing more efficient is not important, nor is the argument that information is needed for a report. Reports can be reconstructed after the fact. The important functions are to deposit cash and to ship product.

EXHIBIT 5.19   Program Development Steps

- Positioning—Make participants feel comfortable with the program development methodology.
- Education—Help participants develop the proper perspective.
- Develop flexible "what if" interim processing strategies.
- Documentation and publishing—Keep it concise and easy to understand.

Protect Ongoing Needs

Users are often reluctant to admit that they could do without certain systems during a stabilization period because they are concerned that their admission might be construed to mean that such systems are not needed during normal operations and could be eliminated.

Emphasize the Low Probability of a Major Disaster

Most managers will never be involved in a major disaster; minor operating inconveniences, perhaps, but not a major long-term outage. It is important to emphasize continually the *extremely* low probability of a major disaster.

Link Low Probability with the Need for Low-Cost, Simple Solutions

It is important to emphasize repeatedly the low probability of a disaster and to remind department managers that they have a responsibility to search for "what if" interim processing strategies.

Analyze Alternate Interim Processing Options

It is helpful to have a list of possible alternate strategies in hand before meeting with users. Take time, in a relaxed atmosphere, to help users brainstorm possible conceptual solutions without worrying about how they might be accomplished. Many times you will end up taking parts of one idea and combining it with another to arrive at a final solution. Unless you go through the process of airing conceptual solutions in a nonthreatening environment, they may never surface. See Exhibit 5.20 for a list of issues that should be covered during this process.

EXHIBIT 5.20 Phase I—Key Tasks

- Identify vital records required to support essential business functions.
- Identify processing requirements necessary to maintain cash flow and service customers.
- Evaluate alternate management practices.
- Identify key management reports.
- Identify systems support personnel.
- Identify primary users.
- Develop interim processing strategies.

Developing "What If" Interim Processing Strategies

The development of alternate interim processing strategies requires analyzing technology dependencies in detail, observing unique operating characteristics, and identifying essential processing requirements. This is a highly specialized process that continually stresses the importance of concentrating on essential business functions and vital records.

Identify Vital Records

During a stabilization period, the concern is not with systems but only with vital records. Most systems contain 85 percent extraneous data that is not essential to survival for short periods of time. This is why it is counterproductive to discuss systems with users. Instead, discussion should be limited to vital records because they constitute the bottom line. If users start to talk in terms of systems, the discussion must be directed back to vital records. *In no instance should a system be the focus.* Systems are a luxury; vital records are a necessity.

Evaluate Proposed Interim Processing Strategies

Management practices often become dependent on computer systems to the extent that it is hard to think of operating without them. However, this issue must be addressed because the use of different management techniques can often compensate for lack of systems support. Department managers should be encouraged to think of methods that could be used temporarily.

Finalize Interim Processing Strategies

The ultimate goal is to develop alternate interim processing strategies that describe how essential business functions will operate until lost work space or technology is restored. Alternate interim processing strategies reflect alternate management practices that department heads are willing to invoke for a short period of time, the acceptance of a temporary loss of efficiency, and a focus only on business functions that have a direct bearing on either cash flow or customer service. See Exhibit 5.21 for a list of activities that should be covered.

EXHIBIT 5.21   Phase II—Key Tasks

- Encourage users to accept primary responsibility for business continuation planning.
- Document exposure to disaster situations.
- Review departmental use of computer systems.
- Review backup procedures.
- Review systems level documentation.
- Document computer hardware specifications.
- Document teleprocessing network specifications.
- Evaluate the risk to essential business functions.
- Analyze interim processing strategies to serve customers and support essential business functions during a stabilization period.

Obtain Department Managers' Approval of Interim Processing Strategies
Department managers must approve the finished product. Input will need editing for consistency in the amount of detail and style of presentation across all business functions. Asking individual departments to document their own strategies may seem logical, but continuity and compatibility may be lacking. Department managers should formulate and be the architects of "what if" interim processing strategies, but *one individual* should control the documentation process. When you think it is presentable, make an appointment with the department manager and review it in as much detail as required. Ask for additions, changes, or corrections; this process will tend to give the department managers ownership in the finished product.

Computer Processing Alternatives

Examples of "what if" interim processing strategies follow.

Accounts Payable
Strategy

- Match receiving reports to invoices manually.
- Selectively approve invoices with large discounts.
- Defer other payments until computer processing capability is restored.
- Prepare checks manually.

Accounts Receivable
Strategy

- Prepare a short list of problem credit accounts; manually analyze and approve credit.
- Automatically approve other orders from existing customers up to a specified limit.
- Approve new customer orders manually.
- Apply cash after computer processing capability is restored.

Billing
Strategy

- Invoice large dollar amounts manually.
- Defer other invoicing until computer processing capability is restored.

Cost Accounting
Strategy

- Collect raw cost accounting data manually.
- Prepare cost accounting reports after computer processing capability is restored.

Customer Service
Strategy

- Refer to the latest hard copy of job status.
- Explain to customers that the computer system is down, but that you will check the status of their orders and call them back.
- Use standard production times for standard products and consult experienced process control personnel for estimated delivery times for special orders.

Engineering
Strategy

- Use aperture cards to view engineering change orders.
- Process changes manually that will have an impact on work-in-process.
- Implement critical work-in-process changes manually.

Fixed Assets
Strategy

- Maintain manual log of transactions during the interim processing period.
- Update records and prepare reports when computer processing capability is restored.

General Ledger
Strategy

- Obtain copies of the most recent financial statements.
- If an outage occurs during the closing cycle, use top-line estimates to close the books or defer closing until computer processing capability is restored.

Human Resources
Strategy

- Defer employee status and salary changes until computer processing capability is restored.
- Make retroactive salary adjustments after computer processing capability is restored.

Inventory Management
Strategy

- Use a computer service bureau to print a copy of the prior day's computer record of inventory status.
- Use a PC spreadsheet to maintain a net balance of inventory receipts and disbursements during the interim processing period.
- Intentionally overorder "B" and "C" items to prevent stock-outs. Plan to work off excess inventory later.
- Monitor and reorder "A" items manually.
- Update computer records for transactions during the stabilization period.

Material Requirements Planning
Strategy

- Operate using the latest hard-copy master schedule, making selected adjustments manually.

- Intentionally overorder "B" and "C" items with the expectation of working off excess inventory later.
- Manually review the impact of new requirements and changes, and selectively order additional "A" items as deemed necessary.

Order Processing
Strategy

- Use fax or phone to receive electronic data interchange (EDI) orders.
- Write new orders manually.
- Prepare copies for order picking or production scheduling.
- Copy and mark up previous order routings for similar orders.
- Use the latest copy of order status report combined with actual shop floor visits to update the status of work-in-process.

Payroll
Strategy

- Store the most recent backup copy of payroll check images off-site.
- Obtain the latest copy of payroll check images and use local computer utility to produce duplicate copies of those checks.
- Prepare checks for new hires and remove checks for terminations manually.
- Include a notice with payroll checks indicating that shortages or averages will be corrected after normal processing capability is restored.

Production Scheduling
Strategy

- Obtain the latest hard copy of the master schedule and the detailed production schedule.
- Prepare move tickets manually as needed.
- Manually update the latest detailed production schedule.

Purchasing
Strategy

- Update the latest hard copy of material status manually.
- Prepare purchase orders manually.

- Prepare copies of purchase orders for receiving.
- Expedite manually.

Receiving
Strategy

- If necessary, use "no P.O." (purchase order) procedures to receive material.
- Use a copy of the packing list to document receipt.
- Record receipts manually on a backup form.
- Send a copy of each receipts form to accounts payable for approval of invoices.

Shipping
Strategy

- Use a copy of the order to set up transportation.
- Prepare bills of lading manually.
- Use similar prior shipment records to develop routing.

Documentation

Documentation review and publishing constitute the next phase. This involves translating alternate interim processing strategies into a program tailored to the operating needs of an organization (see Exhibit 5.22). The objective is to produce a concise deliverable document that

EXHIBIT 5.22   Program Documentation Sections

- Policy
- Strategy
- Executive summary
- Prevention
- Incident recovery
- Interim processing

can be easily used as a reference should an actual disaster occur. Recommended section headings for a program, with suggested wording to serve as a starting point, follow.

Policy

The objectives of a contingency program are to provide an organized response to an isolated disaster that would render communications, computers, or facilities inoperable or inaccessible and to prevent a significant deterioration in either cash flow or the ability to service customer orders during a stabilization period.

Strategy

The strategy of a contingency program is to:

- Ensure that all relevant computerized software and databases are duplicated and stored in a secure off-site location for use in recovery.
- Provide interim processing strategies to support key business functions and maintain market share during a stabilization period.
- Publish a document that can be used as a reference should a disaster actually occur.
- Address environmental and systems changes.

See Exhibit 5.23 for an example of policy and strategy.

Executive Summary

This contingency program is primarily designed to protect against the sudden loss of telephone service, computer processing capability, or access to vital facilities. A disaster might be caused by an incident such as accidental fire, arson, contamination by hazardous material, aircraft accident, tornado, or earthquake. Experience indicates the probability of such a disaster's occurring at a given installation is extremely remote. However, owing to present and planned dependency on technology and vital facilities, "what if" interim processing strategies have been developed to protect market share and to ensure that critical business functions can continue to operate until processing capability is restored.

EXHIBIT 5.23   Policy and Strategy—Examples

Policy

The contingency program policy is to (1) ensure an organized and effective response to an isolated disaster that would render telephone communications, remote data communications, and/or computer equipment inaccessible or inoperative, or normal work locations inaccessible, and (2) ensure business continuity for business functions dependent on computer technology until normal operations are restored.

Strategy

1. Ensure that all relevant computer software and data bases are duplicated and stored in a secure off-site location for use in recovery.
2. Provide interim processing strategies to support essential business functions and maintain cash flow during a computer disaster recovery period.
3. Publish a document that can be used as a reference should a disaster actually occur.
4. Identify responsibility to restore voice communications in the event of a loss of telephone service.
5. Provide for program maintenance for environmental and systems changes.

Prevention

This phase of the program addresses normal operating practices that will be followed to provide an accurate and timely starting point should original data be lost or destroyed. It assigns direct responsibility for specific actions that should be institutionalized into existing position descriptions. The prevention section also provides for periodic testing of alternate interim processing strategies capability.

See Exhibit 5.24 for an example of a prevention program.

Incident Recovery

Although a thorough analysis of operating needs has categorized systems into critical and noncritical categories, the specifics of a recovery program can be determined only at the time of an actual disaster. This depends on the nature of the disaster, the point in time when the disaster occurs, and the anticipated period of disruption. Interim processing strategies activation and definition require a global knowledge of management information systems (MIS) and control of system support

EXHIBIT 5.24 Prevention Program—Examples

Prevention programs outline tasks and responsibilities necessary to support and maintain an effective ongoing contingency program before a localized disaster occurs.

Responsibility	*Action*
Operations Manager	Ensure that all relevant files and databases are consistently backed up in accordance with the processing frequency indicated on application data sheets.
Senior Operator	Rotate magnetic tapes representing databases and data sets based on existing daily, weekly, and monthly schedules to the off-site location.
Operations Manager	Store source programs, compiled programs, operating systems, data communication, and related system software at the off-site location.
	Maintain up-to-date documentation to support production scheduling and computer operations at the off-site location.
	Maintain current applications data entry procedures and program documentation at the off-site location.

resources. The incident recovery section identifies required tasks and responsibilities, such as ordering replacements for damaged equipment and coordinating user processing activities.

See Exhibit 5.25 for an example of incident recovery.

Interim Processing Period
The interim processing period represents the time during which interim processing strategies will be used to protect market share and provide support to vital business functions.

1. *Profile*
   - *System or functional name.* Gives the name of the business function or system being addressed.
   - *System or functional description.* Includes a description of the highlights and major activities of the business function or computer system being addressed.
   - *Key reports.* Lists the major reports used to administer the specific activity.

EXHIBIT 5.25	Incident Recovery

Incident recovery identifies required tasks and responsibilities that must be addressed at the time a specific disaster occurs or are needed to establish temporary data processing capability at another location. It contains actions assigned to specific individuals as well as to an emergency response team who may perform individually or collectively during the stabilization period, at the discretion of the information systems manager.

Responsibility	Action
Information Systems Manager	Determine whether the disaster recovery and business continuation strategies will be activated. Notify appropriate personnel.
Operations Manager	Initiate any reconstruction that might be required at a temporary data processing location.
	Document a chronological list of all key events surrounding the disaster emergency response actions and interim processing activities.
	Instruct user department managers to execute plans for implementing business continuity strategies.
	Notify proper authorities, such as police and fire department, based on the nature of the disaster.
	Expedite installation of new telephone/communications systems as required.

- *Inquiry capability.* Highlights the need to access information for either customer or management needs.
- *Dependencies.* Reflects other business functions or systems that are normally dependent on input from this activity.

See Exhibit 5.26 for an example of a system profile section.

2. *"What If" Interim Processing Strategies*

- *Start-up.* Indicates steps that need to be taken to make the transition from business as usual processing to alternate methods processing during a stabilization period.
- *Interim processing.* Highlights activities that need to be done to support the alternate processing methods. Specifically *how*

EXHIBIT 5.26   System Profile—Example

System name: <u>Accounts Payable</u>

System description:

    This system facilitates vouchering of approved invoices and check processing. The system also permits on-line generation of checks for COD deliveries.

Key reports:

    Checks

    Check register

    Transaction log

On-line inquiry capability:

    Invoice status

Applications dependent on output from this system:

    General ledger

    Purchasing

---

they will be performed is not to be included as long as the functional manager is confident that those details can be easily worked out when they are needed.

- *Records retention.* Indicates those transactions that should be saved so that computer data bases can be updated when normal processing capability is restored.

See Exhibit 5.27 for an example of interim processing strategies.

Maintenance, Preparedness Reviews, and Testing

Because contingency programs are environmentally dependent, effective maintenance, periodic preparedness reviews, and testing are important. Their purpose is to:

- Ensure viability of alternate interim processing strategies through an ongoing awareness and education program and periodic preparedness evaluations.
- Update and maintain contingency plans for systems changes, hardware upgrades, and assigned responsibilities.
- Test backup computer processing capability.

EXHIBIT 5.27   Interim Processing Strategies—Example

System name: <u>Accounts Payable</u>

A. Start-Up

The following step should be taken in anticipation of implementing interim processing strategies:

- Instruct plant and mill locations to pay invoices manually.

B. Interim Processing

The following are processing strategies that will be in effect until normal computer processing is restored:

- Accounts payable pays selected vendor invoices manually to maximize discount allowances.
- Trader offices prepare vendor checks manually.

C. Restoration of computerized data

Records of the following business transactions should be retained so that data files can be updated when normal computer processing is restored:

- Manual checks

Cost Benefits

The cost benefits attributable to this process for program development are primarily the result of the awareness and education module that precedes the business impact analysis. Most other "methodologies" use a business impact analysis to justify the cost of unneeded redundant computer processing capability. This process uses awareness and education to instill in the minds of functional managers the need to search for the most cost-effective solutions. Cost benefits fall into five categories:

1. Lower program development cost
2. Lower backup communications cost
3. Minimization/avoidance of backup computer subscription fees
4. Lower program maintenance cost
5. Lower testing cost

Lower Program Development Costs

The cost of developing a contingency program is directly related to the program development strategy. If you fail to contain scope; determine in advance how much detail is appropriate; conduct an awareness and education program before performing a business impact risk analysis; or insist that first-line supervisors be the architects of interim processing strategies, then costs will soar unnecessarily and the quality of the deliverable document will be greatly compromised.

Lower Backup Communications Costs

In the business as usual mind-set, on-line telecommunications capability is indispensable. In the survival mind-set, it is a luxury. The key is the implementation of an awareness and education program *before* a risk analysis is conducted, so that answers and solutions are pursued within the proper mind-set. Ask remote computer users the right question: "If the computer were operational, but data communications lines were not working, how could you continue to operate?" Although it would be inconvenient and inefficient, most users would come to the conclusion that they *could* use telephones, fax machines, or overnight mail to submit and receive system inquiries. This can avoid the necessity of installing and maintaining backup data communications network capability in the event of a communications failure. It will also help to get remote users back on their feet following a computer disaster during which hardware is operational but the restoration of the communications network may take a few more weeks.

Minimization/Avoidance of Backup Computer Subscription Fees

Most MIS directors are reasonably confident that, given unlimited resources to expedite delivery, authorization to schedule overtime work, and a designated location where they would be permitted to install temporarily a replacement computer, they could restore a mainframe computer operation within a 5- to 10-day period. This extremely important information should be communicated to users during the awareness and education program before conducting a risk analysis. Without this information, users may insist that they could not go more than three days without computer processing. The key to avoiding excessive backup computer subscription fees is to define the "window" *first*. Unless users have this information, their responses to the questions "What is critical?" "How long can you do without?" or "What do you need?" can result in backup computer subscription fees that could have been avoided.

Lower Program Maintenance Costs

Lower program maintenance cost is really a function of avoiding unnecessary detail, because the more detail a program contains, the more costly it is to maintain. Be skeptical of computerized business continuity planning programs, as most encourage an inordinate amount of unnecessary detail. Internal auditors are aware that excessive detail is the downfall of many programs. No one reads such documents; they are not maintained; and organizations have to redo them every three to five years. Keep it simple, avoid unnecessary detail, and the program will live—with less maintenance.

Lower Testing Costs

The simpler the program, the lower the testing cost. Complicated interim processing strategies force unnecessarily complex testing programs. The results are usually frustrating and depressing. Testing is emphasized because auditors know users have little knowledge of what their responsibilities would be during a stabilization period. As a result, auditors insist on testing as a way to force user involvement. The need to test or to periodically examine the viability of proposed interim processing strategies will never be completely eliminated. However, auditors' insistence on testing will decrease once they discover that users are the architects of a program. See Exhibit 5.28 for a list of cost benefits.

Corporate Benefits

Two benefits of the program development process are that it produces a business solution rather than a technical one, and it encourages func-

---

EXHIBIT 5.28   Cost Benefits

- Lower program development cost
- Lower backup communications cost
- Minimization/avoidance of computer hot-site/cold-site subscription fees
- Lower program maintenance cost
- Lower testing cost

tional managers to accept responsibility for contingency planning. These corporate benefits fall into four categories:

1. Sound strategy for program development.
2. Focus is on keeping the business running.
3. Auditors are supportive.
4. Resolves what is critical.

Sound Strategy for Program Development

The primary reason that many organizations do not adequately address a contingency program is that it represents unfamiliar territory. They are not comfortable looking into the abyss. When executives are uncomfortable about an issue, they tend to find a rationale for delaying action. They are particularly reluctant to commit significant resources to a *detailed plan* for an event of which the scope and dimensions are unclear. If you make it clear that your strategy is to make certain that the window is realistic, that the program will concentrate only on business functions that have a significant impact on cash flow and servicing customer orders, and that the intent is to avoid unnecessary detail, then executives will feel comfortable and be supportive.

Focus Is on Keeping the Business Running

Although the need to recover technology is understood, the importance of documenting how business continuity will be maintained during a stabilization period is the primary purpose of a program. This process continually focuses on business continuity and uses essential business requirements to prioritize recovery operations.

Auditors Are Supportive

Directors of internal audit are supportive of the program development process described here, not only because it focuses on business continuity and solves the problem at the business unit level, but because it also emphasizes the avoidance of unnecessary detail. Directors of internal audit know that excessive detail discourages maintenance and causes a program to become obsolete before its time.

EXHIBIT 5.29   Corporate Benefits

- The focus of the program development methodology is on keeping the business running.
- Business continuity is ensured until temporary processing capability is restored.
- Business continuity is ensured between the time temporary processing is restored and the time when communications networks are operational.
- Mission critical business functions are protected.

Resolves What Is Critical

The only way to determine what is critical is to guide users through a process that presents a reasonable window of outage and forces analysis and selection of cost-effective options to support vital business functions until temporary processing capability can be restored. The residual of that process is what is critical. Questionnaires are ineffective in determining what is critical, because of the absence of a sound problem-solving process. See Exhibit 5.29 for a list of corporate benefits.

IMPLEMENTATION

Tailor Presentations

Because contingency planning is done infrequently, it is important to review responsibilities for which key groups should be held responsible—before engaging in formal presentations or discussions. Asking senior management to be responsible for issues that should be dealt with at the department manager level can be embarrassing in any of several ways. Senior management staff may refuse to do it, may send you in the wrong direction, or may give you a wrong answer. Take time to make certain that you are not about to ask any of the groups discussed in the sections that follow to be involved in a process to which it has nothing of substance to contribute.

Role of Senior Management

Senior management has three responsibilities:

1. Make certain that the contingency program policy supports the business plan.
2. Insist that low-probability translates into low-cost solutions.
3. Support the implementation strategy.

Contingency planning will always take last place in a competition of priorities. Left alone, it will never be done. Giving only lip service without the allocation of resources to get the job done will result in a permanently stalled project. Contingency planning works best when chief executive officers issue a written memorandum stressing the need for interim processing strategies, place responsibility for implementation on business unit managers, set a deadline for completion, and approve required resources. Exhibit 5.30 outlines the major role of senior management in the implementation of a contingency program.

Role of a Steering Committee

One of the best ways to garner and sustain support for developing a contingency program is to establish a steering committee (see Exhibit 5.31). The benefit is a group of senior management staff who:

*   Endorse the taking of preventive measures to minimize the likelihood of a disaster.
*   Agree that steps should be taken to minimize the impact on business continuity if a disaster does occur.

EXHIBIT 5.30   Role of Senior Management

*   Approve policy statement.
*   Emphasize importance of cost-effective solution.
*   Support project strategy and methodology.

EXHIBIT 5.31   Role of a Steering Committee

- Provide accountability.
- Provide forum to discuss strategic and tactical issues.
- Assist in conflict resolution.

- Recognize the need to establish strategies that would ensure an organized response to a disaster and the ability to stay in business during a stabilization period.

A steering committee should function only during program development and should be disbanded when the program is complete.

A steering committee has three responsibilities:

1. Serve as an advisory group on program development strategy and methodology.
2. Recommend policy changes.
3. Encourage department managers to participate in the program development process.

Meetings with a steering committee should always be brief and not get bogged down in details. Meetings should not be held on a scheduled basis, but called only when there is something of substance to discuss. A steering committee should not have less than three, nor more than six, members. Representatives from these areas should be considered for membership: finance, operations, auditing, management information systems, and executive.

Role of Department Managers

Department managers, important players in program development, need to participate in an awareness and education program. They are important because they are responsible for approving "what if" interim processing strategies, the heart of any worthwhile contingency program (see Exhibit 5.32). In most instances, the place to find solutions is not with department managers, because they have been removed from the firing line too long. However, their permission and cooperation

EXHIBIT 5.32   Role of Department Managers

- Endorse program philosophy.
- Participate in program development strategy.
- Orient department supervisors.
- Provide access to first-line supervisors.
- Review and approve interim processing strategies.

are needed to work with their first-line supervisors. Never ask a department manager, "What is critical?" The answer, in many instances, will be either inaccurate or incomplete. Nor should one ask how long the department could get along without computer processing capability. They consider computer technology a resource to which they are entitled and are likely to suggest that operating without it for any reason is absurd.

Role of First-Line Supervisors

First-line supervisors are the key to success because they know the territory and are usually willing to listen to new ideas (see Exhibit 5.33). They will take time to understand that redundancy is normally not a cost-effective solution. Their resourcefulness is what you need for success. Take time to educate first-line supervisors about the low probability of a disaster and encourage them to explore various alternatives to normal operating procedures. Encourage them and praise their contribution. Remember that everyone has an ego and likes to be praised for a job well done. Contingency planning is not a technical issue; it is a "people problem," and the effort made to develop good listening and communication skills will pay large dividends in the quality of a program.

EXHIBIT 5.33   Role of First-Line Supervisors

- Attend awareness and education program.
- Be resourceful.
- Look for simple solutions.
- Challenge assumptions.
- Evaluate all options.

Role of Outside Specialists

The traditional reasons for bringing in outside specialists still hold true: Your organization is running lean and no one has the time to devote to developing a contingency program, and/or the outside expert has a special problem-solving process in which no one in your organization is trained. However, there is a more compelling reason to turn to outside specialists for development of a contingency program. The reason is the need to educate functional managers on the cumulative financial impact of providing redundant operating capability and thereby change their expectations and mindset so that they are willing to participate in a program development process that is not disruptive to operations. Functional managers will accept this educational process from outside specialists but may be uneasy and skeptical about "hidden agendas" when it is presented by internal staff.

It is always wise to consider independent advice and counsel when confronted with decisions about nonrecurring issues, particularly when contracts that result from such a decision commit an organization to significant ongoing expenditures.

There is another very good reason for using outside specialists to develop interim processing strategies. It is the one-time conversion of mind-set that must take place in order for managers and supervisors to make a meaningful contribution to the program development process. Mind-set conversion requires an educational process, which is much more readily accepted when conducted by outside specialists. From that point forward, the program can be maintained in-house. There is simply too much at risk in hidden ongoing expenses to leave the initial development of "what if" interim processing strategies to untrained staff (see Exhibit 5.34).

Develop Program with First-Line Supervisors

Although it is important to discover what is critical, one cannot do this by asking a question. The only way to find out what is critical is through an awareness and education program that positions first-line supervisors to search for alternate solutions and that uses a structured

EXHIBIT 5.34   Role of Outside Specialists

- Recommend solutions used by similar organizations.
- Provide direction and guidance.
- Evaluate existing program.
- Evaluate proposed implementation strategy.
- Recommend proven methodologies.
- Recommend quality assurance milestones.
- Provide awareness and education program.

methodology for systematically reducing the problem to manageable tasks. That is why questionnaires are practically worthless in determining what is critical. It takes a process that challenges technology-dependency assumptions, instills a mind-set that accepts inefficiency as a given during a stabilization period, and encourages a search for cost-effective solutions.

How Long Can You Do Without?

It seems like a logical question, but it is one that will cause more problems than it will solve: How long can you do without? The stabilization period is a relatively short time. Technology will be restored somewhere, somehow, but working conditions may not return to normal for months. Asking this question puts the emphasis on *inconvenience* and *time* instead of on examining alternate *solutions*. It runs the risk of not adequately examining alternatives, because it permits the answer to be a product of a mind-set of business as usual rather than survival.

How Would You Survive?

It is important to ignore the first response when asking the question: "If you had to, how would you survive without the computer for eight working days?" Most functional supervisors will say something like "Impossible—everything we do is on the computer, no one around here knows what to do, much less why we do it. All information is in the computer, and it would be impossible for us to function without it."

What you must realize is that, in most instances, the answer is an emotional response and is probably not true. You must be conditioned to ignore that answer and follow up with: "I know, but if you *had* to, how could you keep things going for a period of eight days?" In most instances, a viable solution will surface. The message is clear: If you press hard enough, most supervisors will find ways to maintain vital business functions until lost technology is restored. It is an iterative process of education, anticipating problems, and communicating with the right people to develop solutions. See Exhibit 5.35 for a graphic representation of this process.

Interim processing strategies tend to fall into three categories:

1. Suspend.
2. Use alternate methods.
3. Require redundant capability.

EXHIBIT 5.35 Implementation Process

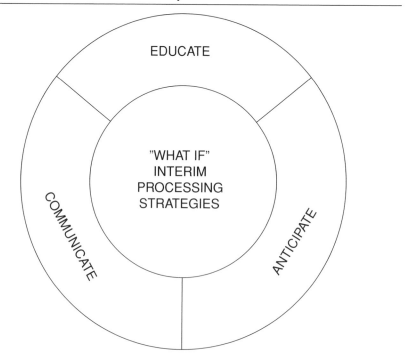

SUSPEND

After considering the high cost of redundancy, the low probability of a disaster's happening, and the relatively brief period before technology is restored, many first-line supervisors will decide to defer processing until technology is restored.

ALTERNATE METHODS

Other first-line supervisors, who are responsible for vital business functions that directly affect either cash flow or customer service, are able to use alternate procedures to get the work done until temporary processing capability is restored.

REQUIRE REDUNDANT CAPABILITY

Some first-line supervisors have determined that there is no conceivable way they can survive without backup processing capability and will normally insist that the backup processing capability be operational in a two- to three-day period. The number of functions that fall into this category should be minimized, as they are the most costly to develop, test, and maintain. Exhibit 5.36 shows the three options available for individual business functions.

Industry Examples

BANKS AND COMMUNICATIONS PROVIDERS

Banks are the exception when it comes to computer contingency planning, because theirs is a transaction-driven business. They need computer hot-site backup so that they can be operational within a 24- to 48-hour time frame.

A category of business that requires even more responsive computer backup capability is that of communications providers, such as telephone companies. They are expected to have instantaneous redundant

---

EXHIBIT 5.36   Three Alternatives

- Suspend processing until normal operations are restored.
- Use nonstandard-practice equipment and procedures during stabilization period.
- Continually fund the cost of redundant processing capability.

processing capability. Most have multiple computers at different locations networked together and designed to pick up the additional load of a failed facility. Because of this system architecture, they do not have exposure to a computer disaster to the extent most other organizations do.

AIRLINES

It might be expected that if any organizations needed redundant computer processing capability, it would be airline reservation systems. However, most major airlines do not have backup processing capability in the event that their centralized computer facility becomes inaccessible or inoperable. Years ago they addressed the problem of single-computer failure by installing backup computers—in the same building. Most have still done nothing to provide backup computer processing in the event that a disaster disables their computer operations. The reason is that it is not cost-effective for them to provide such redundancy.

The reservation system is not the airline industry's primary concern in a disaster. The greatest concern is the maintenance system, because if planes cannot be maintained, they cannot be used to move passengers. The industry is confident that it can operate without a computerized reservation system. Although there may be a drop in customer satisfaction and some people will be forced to take later flights, the airlines do not believe this will have any long-lasting impact on market share. It is a smart decision on their part and one that most businesses should adopt. If a computer disaster is not likely to have any long-lasting or significant impact on market share, then the low probability factor should dictate finding business continuity solutions other than monthly hot-site subscription fees for redundant processing capability. The problem is that most organizations have difficulty disregarding emotions and looking at the issue objectively.

HEALTHCARE

Until recently, healthcare providers had little incentive to pay attention to cost control. They were reimbursed for costs and had no interest in making a profit. Increasingly, however, hospitals, are now paying attention to costs. Most hospitals could admit, treat, perform surgery, prescribe and issue drugs, and discharge patients by using manual procedures for a week or two. Certainly, nurses and administrative support personnel would have to work overtime to keep up with the paperwork. Within a week or two, however, a replacement computer should be operating and ready to assimilate transactions that occurred during a disaster recovery period.

MANUFACTURING

Manufacturing's primary concern is materials management, production, and shipping. Many times this means using computer capability to combine several "like orders" together to eliminate setups and reduce production unit costs and to later be able to reallocate to specific customer orders. Operating without computer processing capability for a few days means orders will be taken manually and copied for use in production and shipment. Manufacturing costs will be excessive and short-term profits will suffer. In the event loss of access to a manufacturing facility occurs, some options to consider are: purchase items normally manufactured, have suppliers perform assembly operations, lease production capacity at other regional locations, outsource operations, and consider other shop routings. Loss of production and distribution facilities has always been a concern, but they are normally protected by business interruption insurance. Another concern is loss of the computer and critical systems, such as order processing and material requirements planning (MRP). Most manufacturing facilities could write orders manually for two weeks and ship from a copy of the handwritten orders. Material requirements planning systems processing could be curtailed for a week or two if necessary; inventory could be intentionally overordered to minimize stock-outs. It is relatively easy to use an off-the-shelf PC program to keep track of receipts and disbursements; the biggest problem is to obtain a beginning balance. One of the more popular solutions is to periodically back up and take off-site a copy of the stock status file. If a disaster does happen, the stock status file is taken to a service bureau and a hard copy is printed to use as a beginning balance.

DISTRIBUTION

Distributors need to be able to take orders, locate and pick items, and ship orders to customers. Working for a few days without computer processing capability presents inventory problems, most of which can be overcome with some preplanning. Make believe a computer disaster has just occurred, and it will be ten days before computer processing capability will be restored. It is obvious that orders normally entered directly into computer systems can be handwritten and that hand-written orders could be used as picking documents. If everything is normally on-line and there are no paper status reports, the problem is knowing where inventory is located, particularly in a dynamic slot-ting environment, and knowing how much of that inventory is available and how much has already been allocated. These two vital starting points of information could be made available immediately following a computer disaster if data processing, as part of a risk management program, stored a snapshot of the inventory locator file and the inventory status file off-site. Immediately following the disaster, those two files could be taken to another compatible computer configuration and printed as a starting point in resuming operations. Future inventory receipts, disbursements, and allocations could be maintained manually or on a PC until computer processing capability is restored.

Loss of access to a distribution facility causes other concerns, such as identifying and replacing inventory that may be damaged or inaccessible and temporarily operating from another location. The snapshots of inventory status mentioned in the previous paragraph will prove helpful in documenting loss to an insurance carrier. The risk management program for a distributor should also provide for maintaining a list of available alternate sites at an off-site location. Drop-shipping is also an alternative.

INSURANCE COMPANIES

Insurance companies operating without on-line computers for several days pose concerns unique to that type of business—how to prevent paying claims on policies that had been canceled; how to direct payments to the correct beneficiary when there may have been a change. There are other issues, but these are the most prominent. Assume that, even without a computer hot-site agreement, computer operations will be resumed at another location within 10 working days. In many instances, it would be another site owned by the same company, in others a "cold site" where temporary computer operations could be set up quickly. The question then becomes: "How do we operate during those 10 days?" Payment of most claims could be delayed for 10 days, which leaves primarily death benefits that should be paid sooner. Again, 10 days is not an unreasonable period to delay payment to ensure that policies are "in-force" and to verify beneficiary data.

Obtain Department Managers' Approval

If care is taken in presenting proposed solutions to department managers, this part of the process normally goes smoothly. Make certain to explain *again* the low probability factor, the high cost of providing redundancy, and the relatively brief stabilization period. In most instances, department managers will approve interim processing strategies with only minor changes. The key is not to be reactionary but to let the first-line supervisor and manager talk it out. Solutions developed by competent first-line supervisors are seldom reversed by department managers.

Present Findings

Findings and recommendations should be presented to senior management in a meeting of no longer than 20 minutes. Take a few minutes to reiterate the low probability factor and the need for low-cost solutions. Impress on this group that the objectives of protecting cash flow and ensuring customer service can be maintained during a disaster recovery period. Summarize the program development strategy and methodology. Present a copy of the completed program for each attendee and *very briefly* review solutions for the top two or three business functions. Thank all present for their support and guidance and be prepared to answer questions. Leave promptly, with the confidence that you have done the job right.

Noncomputerized Business Functions

Just as the loss of computerized operating instructions is avoided by periodically storing them off-site in a secure location, similar protection for procedures performed manually is also necessary. The first objective is to guard against the loss of standard operating procedures (SOP) as a result of a fire or a similar disaster. The recommended process for developing alternate business continuity strategies for non-computerized activities is to:

- Identify all business functions.
- Make copies of all processing instructions.
- Store duplicate instructions off-site.
- Develop an inventory of all documents processed in a noncomputerized mode.
- Identify the *vital* information contained in those documents.
- Identify alternate sources from which vital information could be obtained if the documents are destroyed or become inaccessible.
- Provide backup copies for all others, and store off-site.

Telephones

There have been a sufficient number of incidents of telephone failure and recovery to build a solid case for relying on the utility to restore service in a matter of hours or, at the worst, in a day or two. Utilities operate in the "real-time" mode of disaster recovery; they are always prepared for emergency response and restoration of service. They study, practice, and train specifically for different types of disasters, and they are good at it. Yet there are exceptions. You might want to keep a list of employees who have personal cellular phones that could be pressed into service if needed. Establish concurrence on how and where incoming calls would be routed temporarily and how this information would be communicated to customers. Building and maintaining your own redundant communications capability just for disaster recovery is usually not cost-effective.

Buildings

The options for planning in the event of loss of vital facilities are not many. It is certainly not realistic nor cost-effective to build additional production facilities, distribution centers, or administrative offices just to guard against disasters. The only practical solution for manufacturing and production facilities is to rent capacity from similar businesses until a disabled facility is repaired or replaced. If only standard-practice equipment is destroyed, the choice is either to use nonstandard-practice processes or to sublet those operations to the same organizations used to relieve capacity problems. The usual answer for disabled distribution centers is to temporarily switch demand to another center or to lease public warehouse space.

MAINTENANCE AND TESTING

Objectives

Because contingency programs are environmentally dependent, effective maintenance, continuing education, and preparedness reviews are needed. Their purpose is to:

- Ensure viability of "what if" interim processing strategies through a program of continuing education and preparedness evaluation.
- Update and maintain contingency plans for systems changes, hardware upgrades, and assigned responsibilities.
- Test backup technology.

Maintenance

Systems and procedural changes should be reviewed quarterly to ensure that new customer services or modifications to existing services have not invalidated alternative interim processing strategies. They should be reviewed with data processing personnel to make certain that computer recovery plans are compatible with these strategies.

Reviews should also be conducted to ensure awareness of data processing responsibilities during normal operations, emergency response, and stabilization periods.

Prevention

Activities included in this section form the foundation on which much of the program is based. There is a great deal of dependency on this section. Annual reviews should be scheduled to examine and update procedures and personnel assignments to prevent the program from deteriorating and becoming obsolete.

Incident Response
An annual meeting should be scheduled to ensure that promotions and attrition have not affected assigned responsibilities.

Interim Processing
Interim processing strategies should be reviewed annually to ensure that new customer services or modifications to existing services have not invalidated these strategies. The interim processing strategies should in turn be reviewed with the data processing department to make certain that computer processing continues to be compatible with capacities and capabilities.

Continuing Education and Preparedness Reviews

To ensure that a program is workable, individuals need to be aware of their responsibilities and prepared to implement them in the event of a disaster. Through a continuing program of education, periodic preparedness review, and evaluation, user awareness can be maintained.

On a selected basis, functional departments should be examined to determine how prepared they are to cope with an actual disaster. The examination should include, but not necessarily be limited to, these considerations:

- Awareness of the program
- Accessibility of a copy of the program at an off-site location
- Concurrence with specific responsibilities
- Ability to demonstrate how selected interim processing strategies would actually be accomplished

Planning
Prior feedback summaries, as well as the prevention and incident recovery sections of the contingency program, should be reviewed and specific functions selected for examination.

Examination
Meet with selected users and data processing personnel to determine how well prepared they are to cope with an actual disaster. Examination would include, but not necessarily be limited to, these considerations:

- Awareness of the program
- Accessibility of a copy of the program at an off-site location
- Conceptual awareness of specific responsibilities
- The extent to which the contingency program has been kept current
- Strategies for implementing the program

Education
Education is an ongoing process during the examination step. It consists of reviewing the intent of the program, explaining terminology, and recommending various techniques or strategies that might be helpful.

Feedback
Summarize problems and deficiencies and provide specific direction for corrective action.

Technology Testing

The purpose of testing is to assess specific hardware and/or software capabilities of computers. Testing should be preceded by planning with users and data processing personnel to select a process for testing of the backup computer processing capability.

Testing should include, but not be limited to:

- Accessibility of backup files at an off-site storage location
- Retrieval and copying of backup files
- Establishment of temporary communications lines
- Limited operation of selected user applications

Upon completion of testing, feedback provides a documented summary of deficiencies, accompanied by directions for corrective action.

Planning
Meet with data processing personnel to identify specific hardware and/or software capabilities to be tested. Equally important is to test alternate telecommunication links sufficiently to ensure that they can be made operational in the anticipated time frame and that sufficient

load is simulated to be reasonably confident that the actual demand can be handled during a stabilization period.

Meet with functional department heads to encourage them to participate in testing and to work with them in defining what should be expected from the test. The objective of a true test should not be to see whether the computer runs, but to have the functional business units actually process test data and verify that the results of the test are complete and accurate. The business units should define what constitutes a successful test, not the data processing department. Initially, it is acceptable to notify personnel ahead of time so that they are sufficiently prepared to test; however, as time goes on, it is important to spring some surprise tests just to keep people alert and aware that if the real thing happens, this is the way it will be.

Conducting the Test

Testing backup computer processing capability should, as a minimum, provide verification that the proper files and databases are being stored offsite, that applications can be restored, and that transactions can be processed properly. To accomplish these testing goals at a computer hot site means actually operating the backup computer at the hot site with your own staff. It can be an expensive procedure but a necessary one if redundant processing capability is your strategy. Whatever your solution is, it should be testable. This is a problem with a cold-site strategy.

The basic difficulty with a computer cold-site solution is that it is not practical to test. Cold-site testing would mean having to:

- Have a replacement computer delivered to a cold site.
- Have the computer installed and made operational.
- Repeat the hot-site testing process previously discussed.
- Return the computer to the vendor and expect the vendor to be able to sell it to someone else as new equipment.

Because a cold-site strategy is for all intents and purposes untestable, it is not a viable solution. The recommended solution is either a computer hot site or a business continuity program that stipulates how essential business functions that are normally dependent on computer processing can survive until computer processing capability is restored.

Feedback Summaries

The first suggestion is that a summary of test results can be prepared not by data processing, but by functional business unit managers. The feedback summary should state the purpose of the test, the specific *measurable* test goals that were established by the business unit managers, the extent to which these goals were achieved, and what corrective action is recommended—including the name of the person responsible for the corrective action and the date by which it should be completed. Previous feedback summaries should be examined at the time a test is planned to ensure that the problem areas remain in order.

6

GUIDELINES FOR DEVELOPING CONTINGENCY PROGRAMS AT MULTIPLE LOCATIONS

BACKGROUND

Providing quality solutions to multiple problems is the goal. This emphasis on quality control manifests itself in methods standards and performance standards. The objective of these standards is to ensure consistency in data gathering, codification and classification, processing, and report preparation.

Contingency planning or, more specifically, contingency program planning, constitutes one of the major fields of practice. This specialty is destined to grow in demand and complexity. Much of the growth is the result of increased dependence on computerized systems. The complexity issue is a direct result of the technology explosion.

OBJECTIVES AND SCOPE

Guidelines for Developing Contingency Programs for Multiple Locations were developed to provide methods and performance standards in developing, maintaining, and testing contingency programs. They have been developed to help companies control program development costs while ensuring quality in deliverables. They also contain standards for evaluating staff performance.

Section I recommends organization of the contingency planning function. It also emphasizes the importance of senior management's involvement in defining corporate contingency program policy and strategy.

Section II provides guidelines in project implementation planning. It establishes standards for evaluating environments, identification of unique requirements, and developing a cost-effective implementation strategy.

Section III covers methods and staff performance standards for developing "what if" interim processing strategies for use during a stabilization period immediately following a disaster. Emphasis is on departmental managers' involvement.

Section IV provides methods and staff performance standards for documenting facility contingency programs. Risk management program documentation format is defined as "procedural"; emergency response is defined as "checklist"; and interim processing strategies are defined as "guidelines."

Section V covers institutionalizing program maintenance and testing. It also covers conducting compliance audits to encourage continued preparedness.

SECTION I: ORGANIZATION

Placement of the Contingency Planning Activity

An increasing dependency on computerized on-line systems and vital facilities underlines the need to place responsibility for data security and disaster recovery responsibilities properly within a company's organization. This is important when one considers that disasters such as fire, explosion, or sabotage can leave facilities inaccessible for several weeks.

It should be emphasized that the real issue in contingency planning is development of practical and workable "what if" interim processing strategies. These strategies accomplish two objectives during a stabilization period immediately following a disaster:

1. Protect market share
2. Provide continuity in servicing customers

Development of a contingency program is really a type of long-range strategic planning. Although the probability of having to activate interim processing strategies is extremely remote, there is no doubt it is a strategic planning issue for most companies. It is, therefore, a corporate issue, and responsibility for its success does not belong within the data processing function.

It is recommended that responsibility for contingency program development and maintenance be positioned in this way:

- In manufacturing plant locations, it should be a staff position that reports directly to the plant general manager.
- In corporate headquarters, it should be a staff position that reports to the chief operating officer, such as the human resources director.

Organizational Functions

A contingency program developer must be technically competent and have access to all executive management and line management personnel. Moreover, planning, updating existing documentation, staying current with state-of-the-art technology, and supplying reliable information to management involve a high degree of integrity, objectivity, and skill.

The contingency program developer should report to one executive and be responsible for these functions:

- Development
- Implementation
- Testing
- Maintenance

Operational effectiveness of a contingency program is enhanced when sound internal control practices are followed. This is particularly important in developing interim processing strategies for individual departments, in which preparedness depends heavily on familiarity with day-to-day operations.

All persons within the organization should recognize that the contingency program is important. Accordingly, a major effort should be made to ensure that all individuals responsible for this activity can work effectively with all levels of management. They should have both technical and administrative competence, as well as personality characteristics compatible with those of other key individuals in the organization.

The authority and responsibility for functions that must go on during normal operations should be comprehensively documented. These functions provide the foundation required to support emergency response and the alternate operating practices that will be used during a stabilization period. Precise, written instructions should be prepared and circulated to all key individuals. These day-to-day functions, which are critical to the actual recovery from a disaster, should be institutionalized into daily routines.

Responsibility for specific actions that must be accomplished within hours after an actual disaster occurs also need to be cited individually. In addition, a follow-up mechanism to ensure that they have been completed must be documented. Care must be taken to ensure that these functions will still be performed in spite of personnel loss at the time of a disaster.

"What if" interim processing strategies that will be used to maintain business continuity immediately following a disaster must be clearly documented, including specific guidelines that clarify what alternate methods are expected to be used in lieu of standard procedures. Although these strategies need not result in detailed procedures, they should be sufficiently explicit that an individual familiar with a particular function can easily visualize how the alternate methods that are expected to be implemented during a stabilization period can be accomplished.

SECTION II: STANDARDS FOR IMPLEMENTATION PLANNING

Methods Standards

Objective
To provide a checklist and guidelines to follow in conducting the strategic planning phase portion of developing a contingency program.

Review of Environment
Assemble this information through obtaining copies, interviews, observations, and analysis:

- Organization charts of all departments
- Telephone directory
- Copy of outside auditors' and internal auditors' comments on disaster recovery needs

Preliminary Statement of Objectives
- Document:
  - Objectives of executive management
  - Concerns of key executives
  - Constraints or conditions
- Document exposure to disasters:
  - Tornado
  - Fire
  - Flood
  - Explosion
  - Sabotage
  - Aircraft
  - Work stoppage
  - Workplace violence
  - Other
- Review any prior attempts to develop a contingency program:
  - Policy
  - Strategy
  - User participation
  - Procedures:
    - Normal operations
    - Emergency response
    - Stabilization

- Completeness
- Up-to-date
- Testing
- Preparedness
- Identify vital facilities and critical operations concerned with:
  - Market share
  - Customer service
- Observe operating practices.
- Document hardware configuration.
- Document teleprocessing network.
- Review physical security.
- Review data security.
- Examine vital records program.
- Document the cost of any existing or proposed backup processing sites.
- Review existing backup agreements.
- Develop implementation program:
  - Tasks
  - Strategy
  - Timetable
  - Effort

Performance Standards

Objective
To provide measurement and reporting techniques to monitor quality and costs.

Elapsed Time
- Elapsed time commitments will be included in proposals for each phase of an engagement.
- At the first indication that elapsed time commitments contained in a proposal might not be met, it is imperative that a written

memo be delivered to the project director within two working days.

- Elapsed time commitments will be subject to review subsequent to the completion of each phase.

Effort

- Man-hours of effort required to complete these activities are to be reviewed and signature approved by the project director in the "review" copy of the discussion draft proposal:
  - Planning
  - Meetings (including preparation)
  - Data gathering
  - Evaluating and organizing
  - Business continuity strategies
  - Procedure development
  - Review and finalize
- Target (budgeted) man-hours (less any man-hours expended in previous months) will be reflected on the current month's time sheet of the project manager.
- Actual hours expended will be recorded against the activity performed on the proper date on each individual's time sheet.
- The project manager will review budgets and hours expended to date weekly and notify project director in memo form of any expected overruns.

SECTION III: STANDARDS FOR DEVELOPING INTERIM PROCESSING STRATEGIES

Methods Standards

Objective
To provide a checklist and guidelines to follow in developing interim processing strategies.

Methodology

Development of sound, well-thought-out "what if" strategies is without question the most important part of developing a successful contingency program. It is an iterative process that requires you to:

1. *Position* your thinking such that you can feel and visualize the concerns of individual users and take the time through multiple get-togethers (as opposed to formal meetings) to listen carefully to their thoughts.

2. *Anticipate* what the problem areas might be, and then formulate conceptually what options might be available as solutions.

3. *Communicate* with other knowledgeable individuals on a casual basis to check out the various options and to help you begin to formulate the interim processing strategies you would like endorsed.

In conducting the iterative process, be careful to introduce yourself to the department heads before you meet with first-line supervision. In meetings with the department heads, you should:

- Be professional in your conduct.
- Briefly explain the charter of the engagement.
- Mention that contingency planning is a corporate issue and that you expect many of the solutions and answers to be developed while working with first-line supervisors.
- Request permission to contact supervisors to document existing practices and procedures.
- Explain that many times the interim processing strategy that will emerge is a combination of: (1) discontinuing activities that could be done without in a crisis condition; (2) finding alternate methods of obtaining information; and (3) processing data manually until normal processing capability is restored.

It is important to drive home these issues in your discussions with department heads and other users:

- The probability of ever experiencing an actual disaster is extremely remote.

- The charter is *not* concerned with brief outages of a few hours or one or two days.
- There is no insurance available that will cover loss of market share.
- Traditional business functions, such as payroll, invoicing, accounts receivable, and accounts payable, must continue to function.

Performance Standards

Objective
To provide measurement and reporting techniques to monitor quality and costs.

Elapsed Time
- Elapsed time commitments will be included in proposals for each phase of an engagement.
- At the first indication that elapsed time commitment might not be met, it is imperative that a written memo be delivered to the project director within two working days.
- Elapsed time commitments will be subject to review subsequent to the completion of each phase.

Effort
- Targeted (budgeted) man-hours (less any man-hours expended in previous months) will be reflected on the current month's time sheet of the project manager for these activities:
  - Meetings
  - Data gathering
  - Evaluating and organizing
  - Field trips
  - Formulating proposed interim processing strategies
- Actual hours expended will be recorded against the activity performed on the proper date on each individual's time sheet.

SECTION IV: DOCUMENTATION STANDARDS

Methods Standards

Objective
To provide a checklist and guidelines to follow in documenting responsibility for these time periods:

- Prevention
- Incident response
- Interim processing

Methodology
Documentation will be written in this format:

- Step numbers will be assigned chronologically.
- Responsibilities will be assigned to specific job titles.
- Activity statements must begin with an action verb and be concise.

Prevention
These activities should be specifically addressed:

- Letter of understanding for use of a backup computer processing site
- Creation of copies of:
  - Master files
  - Source programs
  - Databases
  - Unprocessed transactions
  - Operating system
- Off-site storage of frequently backed up items
- Creation of latest copies of documentation:
  - Systems documentation
  - Computer operating instructions
- Off-site storage of latest copies of documentation

- Update off-site storage records for current status.
- Off-site storage of special forms
- Alternate input methods for future systems
- Develop specifications for current equipment:
  - Air conditioning
  - Electrical
  - Telephones
  - Communications
- Off-site storage of specifications
- Update contingency program for new systems.
- Test preparedness.
- Test backup site processing.
- Update contingency program for changes.

Incident Recovery
These activities should be specifically addressed:

- Program activation
- Media notification
- Customers notification
- Order replacements for damaged equipment.
- Document historical record of events.
- Provide 24-hour protection at site of disaster.
- Obtain backup copies of:
  - Frequently backed up items
  - Documentation
  - Special forms
  - Specifications
- Copy backup items.
- Return backup items to off-site storage.
- Arrange for physical security and data security.
- Supervise packing and moving of files and equipment.

- Arrange for emergency telephone service.
- Establish processing schedules.
- Arrange for expense advances and payment of current expenses.

"What If" Interim Processing Strategies

These items should be addressed in interim processing strategies:

1. *Loss of data communications*
   - Systems that will continue normal processing (no requirement)
   - Systems that will need minor adjustments in input media to continue normal processing:
     - Specify steps needed to alter input method.
     - Assign specific responsibilities for changing input media.
     - Specify responsibility for accumulating transactions.
     - Specify responsibilities for internal controls.
     - Specify responsibility for updating computer files after normal processing capability has been restored.
     - Specify alternate methods to be used during the stabilization period.
     - Assign responsibility for notifying affected personnel.
     - Assign responsibility for internal controls.
   - Systems that will defer computer processing until after normal processing capability is restored:
     - Specify responsibility for notifying affected personnel.
     - Specify responsibility for accumulating transactions.
     - Specify responsibilities for internal controls.
     - Specify responsibility for updating computer files after normal processing capability has been restored.
   - Functions that will defer computer processing until normal processing capacity is restored and will use alternate methods to support the function:
     - Specify responsibility for notifying affected personnel.

2. *Loss of computer processing capability*
   - Systems that will defer computer processing until normal processing capability is restored:
     - Specify responsibility for notifying affected personnel.
     - Specify responsibility for accumulating transactions.
     - Specify responsibility for internal controls.
     - Specify responsibility for updating computer files after normal processing capability has been restored.
     - Specify alternate methods to be used during the interim processing period.
   - Systems that will process on a backup computer:
     - Specify responsibility for notifying affected personnel.
     - Specify responsibility for accumulating transactions.
     - Specify responsibility for internal controls.
     - Specify responsibility for loading backup files.
     - Specify responsibility for contacting: (1) users, (2) production scheduling, (3) computer operators, and (4) application support personnel.
     - Specify responsibility for implementing alternate procedures for obtaining input.
3. *Loss of facility access*
   - Identify individual business functions.
   - Identify administrative and systems support activities that directly impact market share and customer service.
   - Develop "what if" interim processing strategies for each support activity and business function.

Performance Standards

Objective
To provide measurement and reporting techniques to monitor quality and costs.

Elapsed Time

- Elapsed time commitments will be included in proposals for each phase of an engagement.
- At the first indication that elapsed time commitments might not be met, it is imperative that a written memo be hand-delivered to the project manager within two working days.
- Elapsed time commitments will be subject to review subsequent to the completion of each phase.

Effort

- Targeted (budgeted) man-hours (less any man-hours expended in previous months) will be reflected on the current month's time sheet of the project manager for these activities:
  - Meetings
  - Data gathering
  - Evaluating and organizing
  - Field trips
  - Formulating proposed business continuity strategies
- Actual hours expended will be recorded against the activity performed on the proper date on each individual's time sheet.

SECTION V: STANDARDS FOR ONGOING MAINTENANCE AND TESTING

Methods Standards

Objective

To provide a checklist and guidelines to follow in testing interim processing capability and preparedness of personnel to cope with a disaster condition on a timely basis.

Methodology

- Develop a test program to audit compliance with normal processing procedures for these activities:

- Creating backup files
- Storing backup copies
- Updating documentation
- Updating equipment lists
- Keeping personnel names current
- Updating specifications for current equipment
- Updating manual for new systems
- Document results of the test of preparedness in concise narrative form.
- Develop and document recommendations for improved preparedness.
- Conduct feedback session with affected personnel.
- Conduct follow-up sessions as required.
- Develop a test program that reveals how aware responsible personnel are regarding their specific responsibilities during the stabilization period and how familiar they are with how to carry out these responsibilities for such activities as:
  - Activating the program
  - Notifying personnel
  - Notifying press
  - Notifying customers
  - Ordering replacement equipment
  - Obtaining backup copies
  - Protecting backup copies
  - Arranging for physical security
  - Arranging for emergency telephone service
  - Establishing processing schedules
- Document results of the test in concise narrative form.
- Develop and document recommendations for improved preparedness.
- Conduct feedback sessions.
- Conduct hot-site test and conduct feedback sessions.

Performance Standards

Objectives

- To provide a continuing education process by which preparedness to cope with a disaster situation will be continually improved
- To provide a program to test business continuity strategies

Elapsed Time

- Elapsed time commitments will be included in proposals for each phase of an engagement.
- At the first indication that elapsed time commitments might not be met, it is imperative that a written memo be hand-delivered to the project manager within two working days.
- Elapsed time commitments will be subject to review subsequent to the completion of each phase.

Effort

Targeted (budgeted) man-hours (less any man-hours expended in previous months) will be reflected on the current month's time sheet of the project manager for these activities:

- Meetings
- Data gathering
- Evaluating and organizing
- Field trips
- Formulating proposed interim processing strategies

7

CONCEPTUAL BUSINESS CONTINUITY STRATEGIES FOR LOSS OF COMPUTER OPERATIONS

POLICY AND STRATEGY

Policy

The contingency program policy is to: (1) ensure an organized and effective response to an isolated disaster that would render telephone communications, remote date communications, and/or computer equipment inaccessible or inoperative; and (2) ensure business continuity for business functions dependent on computer technology, until normal computer processing capability is restored.

Strategy

The strategy follows.

- Ensure all relevant computer software and databases are duplicated and stored in a secure off-site location for use in recovery.
- Provide interim processing strategies to support essential business functions and maintain cash flow during a computer disaster recovery period.
- Identify responsibility to restore voice communications in the event of a loss of telephone service.

- Document computer equipment recovery strategy.
- Provide for program maintenance for environmental and systems changes.

EXECUTIVE SUMMARY

The disaster recovery and business continuation program is designed to protect against the sudden loss of telephone communications, data communications, and/or computer processing capability through disasters such as fire, water, explosion, aircraft accident, or sabotage. Experience indicates that the probability that such a disaster might occur to a given installation is extremely remote. However, due to present and planned dependency on computer processing, interim processing strategies have been developed to protect market share and to ensure that critical business functions can continue to operate until computer processing capability is restored.

It is expected that computer operations will be able to be restored within eight working days. In a worst-case scenario, interim processing strategies could be in effect longer. Although temporary discontinuance of some systems may result in a loss of efficiency, the objective is to prevent a significant deterioration in cash flow and/or the ability to service customers during a disaster recovery period.

Following are the different time periods covered by this program.

Normal Operations

This phase of the program addresses normal operating practices that should be followed to minimize the impact of a localized computer disaster and to provide the foundation for an organized response and ensure business continuity during a disaster recovery period. It assigns direct responsibility for specific actions, including periodic testing of user interim processing strategies capability.

Emergency Response

Responsibility to alert senior management of the need to activate this equipment recovery program with the information systems manager or designate.

The specifics of a recovery program can be determined only at the time a disaster occurs. They depend on the nature of the disaster, the point in time that the disaster occurs, and the anticipated period of disruption. Program activation requires global knowledge of management information systems and control of systems support resources.

The emergency response section identifies activities that will need attention immediately following a computer disaster. It is intended to ensure an organized response and to provide a checklist of issues that need attention.

Interim Processing

The interim processing period represents the time during which interim processing strategies will be used to protect market share and provide support to essential business functions. These interim processing strategies and guidelines have been developed by operating personnel who are the ones most knowledgeable concerning their needs and capability to service customers during a computer disaster recovery period.

Maintenance and User Continuing Education and Preparedness Reviews

Because computer disaster recovery and business continuity programs are environmentally dependent, effective maintenance, user continuing education and preparedness reviews, and backup computer testing programs are needed. Their purpose is to:

- Assure viability of user interim processing strategies through a program of continuing education and preparedness evaluation
- Update and maintain contingency programs for systems changes, hardware upgrades, and assigned responsibilities
- Test backup computer processing capability

Maintenance
Systems changes and additions should be reviewed quarterly to ensure that new customer services or modifications to existing services have

not invalidated existing interim processing strategies. These interim processing strategies should be reviewed with data processing to make certain that computer processing plans are compatible with these strategies.

Reviews should also be conducted to ensure awareness of data processing responsibilities during normal operations, emergency response, and interim processing periods.

NORMAL OPERATIONS

Activities in the normal operations section form the foundation upon which much of the program is based. There is a great deal of dependency on this section. Annual reviews should be scheduled to examine and update these procedures/personnel assignments to prevent the program from deteriorating and becoming obsolete.

EMERGENCY RESPONSE

Meetings should be scheduled annually with selected users, systems analysts, and data processing personnel to ensure that promotions and attrition have not affected assigned responsibilities.

INTERIM PROCESSING

Interim processing strategies should be reviewed annually with user departments to ensure that new customer services or modifications to existing services have not invalidated interim processing strategies. These strategies should in turn be reviewed with data processing to make certain that computer processing continues to be compatible with capacities and capabilities.

USER CONTINUING EDUCATION AND PREPAREDNESS REVIEWS

In order to ensure that a program is workable, users need to be aware of their responsibilities and be prepared to implement them in the event of a disaster. Through a continuing program of education, periodic preparedness review, and evaluation, user awareness can be maintained.

On a selected basis, users should be examined to determine how well prepared they are to cope with a computer disaster. The examination should include, but not necessarily be limited to, these considerations:

- Awareness of the program.
- Accessibility to a copy of the program from an off-site location.
- Concurrence with specific responsibilities.
- Ability to demonstrate how selected interim processing strategies would actually be accomplished.

PLANNING
Prior feedback summaries as well as the normal operations, emergency response, and interim processing sections of the disaster recovery program should be reviewed and specific functions selected for examination.

EXAMINATION
Meet with selected users and data processing personnel to determine how well prepared they are to cope with a computer disaster. Examination would include, but not necessarily be limited to, these considerations:

- Awareness of the program.
- Accessibility to a copy of the program from an off-site location.
- Conceptual awareness of specific responsibilities.
- The extent to which the computer recovery program has been kept current.

Education
Education is an ongoing process during the examination step. It consists of reviewing intent of the program, explaining terminology, and recommending various techniques or strategies that might be helpful.

Feedback
Summarize problems and deficiencies accompanied by specific direction for correction action.

GLOSSARY

Business as usual Operating under normal conditions, that is, without any significant interruption of operations as a result of a disaster.

Business continuity strategies Guidelines that outline how specific activities will be performed until normal processing capability is restored and buildings are accessible.

Business function The most elementary activities, for example, calculating gross pay, updating job descriptions, matching invoices to receiving reports.

Business impact analysis A study to estimate the effect that a specific disaster/incident might have on a given operation or activity.

Cold site A backup computer site without computer hardware. All environmental components, such as power, air conditioning, and data communications, are installed. Theoretically, a computer cold site could be operational within a few hours or days following delivery of hardware.

Declaration fee A one-time charge paid to a computer backup hot-site (or cold-site) provider at the time a disaster is officially declared.

Disaster An incident of such severity and magnitude that emergency steps are needed to stay in business.

Contingency program phases Consists of (1) prevention—the period of time before a disaster occurs, (2) incident recovery—the hours or days immediately following a disaster, (3) interim processing—the period of time from the occurrence of a disaster until temporary operations are restored.

First-line supervisor The level of management just above hourly employees or clerical staff.

Hot site   A backup computer site with compatible hardware installed.

Localized disaster   An incident that affects only a single building or area.

Mobile site   Either a hot site or cold site on wheels; usually one or more large trailers.

Normal operations   See *contingency program phases.*

Notification list   A list of key individuals to be contacted, usually in the event of a disaster. Notification lists normally contain phone numbers and addresses, which may be used in the event that telephones are not operational.

Off-site location   A location usually at least several hundred yards or more from a facility that could incur a disaster.

Positioning   The process of making others feel comfortable with your strategy, style, and methodology of contingency plan development.

Reciprocal agreement   When two different organizations mutually agree to back up each other's processing capability in the event that either one incurs a disaster.

Redundant backup site   Any of two or more data centers that could (by temporarily decreasing their own workload) assume the processing load of critical applications from another data center.

Service bureau   A data processing utility that provides processing capability, normally for specialized processing, such as payroll.

Shell facility   See *cold site.*

Stabilization period   The period of time between the occurrence of a disaster and the time when normal operations are restored.

Subscription fee   Normally, monthly fees paid for the privilege of using (for purposes described in this book) a backup computer hot site or cold site, on a first-come, first-served basis.

Vital business functions   Those specific business activities that have a significant impact on cash flow or servicing customer orders.

Window   The length of time it is expected to take (under emergency conditions, with adequate resources) to restore whatever processing capability was destroyed in a disaster.

INDEX